IMAGE OF AMERICA

Our Literature
from Puritanism to the Space Age

by

Norman Foerster

UNIVERSITY OF NOTRE DAME PRESS

NOTRE DAME   LONDON

PREFACE

The object of this small book is to increase the general reader's understanding — and hence enjoyment — of our national literature. The method is to relate the literature to the vital currents of American experience.

As simply and vividly as I could, I have sketched the profound changes, from colonial days to the present, in the outward aspect of life, its social arrangements and manners, its discontents and aspirations, its vision of the nature of man and of human values. Literature comes from life and reflects life, selectively. In reading the literature of the American people one is greatly advantaged by a fresh awareness (to paraphrase the heading of a famous chapter in Thoreau's *Walden*) of "Where They Lived, and What They Lived For."

At first our literature was dominantly religious, "God-centered"; in the eighteenth century, humanistic, "man-centered"; and from then on, more and more "nature-centered." The last of these may be subdivided into phases: first the romantic idealism that usually affirmed a kinship between the outer world and the human spirit; then a down-to-earth realism expressing a new sense of the actual encouraged by frontier raciness and the positive method of science in the age of Darwin; and finally the deepening and darkening of realism, under the influence of naturalistic philosophies and psychologies, from the 1890's to the present searchings for new directions.

Once alert to the life and thought from which, in each period, the literature emerged, the reader is prepared to understand more readily the literary activities and achievements — the aims of movements and schools, the prevailing ideas, forms, and styles, the salient characteristics of a few typical writers, which are described in the last part of each chapter.

N. F.

CONTENTS

                                                                Page

Preface   iii

I   The Puritan Age   1
      The Word of God as the Law of Man

II   The Neo-Classic Age   20
      Human Reason and Natural Order

III   The Romantic Movement   45
      Individualism in Feeling and Imagination

IV   The Rise of Realism   88
      The Texture of Ordinary Living

V   The Realistic Movement and New Directions . . . 115
      Disillusionment and the Search for Values

THE PURITAN AGE
The Word of God as the Law of Man

"Man should not glory in himself, but alone in God"—EDWARDS

The earliest "American" writers were really English. Captain John Smith, William Bradford, John Winthrop, Roger Williams, Anne Bradstreet, Michael Wigglesworth, Edward Taylor, and Samuel Sewall arrived in the New World at an average age of thirty-seven. They were English in birth and culture, as English as their contemporaries abroad, such as the authors of *Paradise Lost* and *The Pilgrim's Progress*. They thought like Englishmen, they wrote about issues of concern in England, they followed English models of literary style. The did not look upon themselves as Americans — a name they sometimes applied to the Indians.

1

The English settled in the South and New England, but between these two regions the land was partly occupied, at first, by immigrants from the European continent. The Dutch, the Swedes, the Finns, the French and others brought various tongues and patterns of living. New Netherland rose in the valley of the Hudson, New Sweden in the valley of the Delaware, though both were presently absorbed by the English. In the first half of the eighteenth century some 80,000 Germans and Swiss and 50,000 Scotch-Irish introduced racial groups destined to play important roles in the development of the country. The Melting Pot began to simmer. With prophetic truth Crèvecoeur observed, by the time of the Revolution, "Here individuals of all nations are melted into a new race of men, whose labors and posterity will one day cause great changes in the world." Religious differences, however, were at best tolerated rather than blended. There were Quakers, Anglicans, Catholics, Lutherans and many others, as well as the Puritans of New England.

THE PURITANS OF NEW ENGLAND

It was the Puritans of the seventeenth century who, more than any other early colonists, affected deeply the national character in later times. And it was they who wrote most of the literature of the first colonial century. These are reasons enough to speak of this century and part of the next as a "Puritan Age."

Why did so many Puritans leave their homes in "the best island in the universe" (the phrase is Cotton Mather's) and begin life over again in a dark primeval forest, establishing the frontier of Europe 3,000 miles across the turbulent Atlantic? Whatever motive we may choose to emphasize, most of them thought of themselves as refugees from tyranny and persecution. Clearly, they were also looking for material advantage. As an English historian, G. M. Trevelyan, weighed their motives, "The desire for free land and economic opportunity was part of the inducement, but would not by itself have filled the wilderness of New England with folk. For when in 1640 the persecution ceased, the immigration thither ceased also." The persecution which they bitterly resented — the efforts of Archbishop Laud to force conformity to his own ideas of church observances — may not seem too shocking to us in our century of the totalitarian state. But the issues at stake seemed pivotal, both to those who stayed in England and helped to bring on civil war, revolution, and the rule of Cromwell, and to those who migrated to America because they were outraged by arbitrary acts and were fearful of the future. The Puritans who settled New England were men of independent stamp who had their full share of the protesting spirit of Protestantism, a spirit dramatized, even two hundred years later, when Emerson resigned his pulpit.

A radical group came first, the small band of Pilgrims who founded Plymouth in 1620. They were poor and humble and devout — "cobblers, tailors, feltmakers, and such-like trash," the bishop of London chose to characterize them. Ten years later came the founders of the Massachusetts Bay Colony, a large band of conservative Puritans, led by landed gentry, wealthy merchants, university graduates. Their fleet of eleven ships carried livestock, tools, and a full assortment of supplies. With them began a great migration that lasted throughout two decades of turmoil in the mother country. During these years (1620-1640) the Puritans spread along the coast from Maine almost to what is now suburban New York. By 1640, when Virginia had 8,000 white people, New England had 14,000, chiefly in Massachusetts. Then the influx of new settlers almost ceased. For the next half century the hardy and prolific Puritans were free to develop their own government, economy, and way of life virtually undisturbed by the authorities in England. After the arrival of a Governor-General in 1686 it began to be clear that the independence they had enjoyed in isolation would have to yield, if gradually, to royal insistence on imperial control. But by this time they had given to New England a special character which in some respects is evident to the present day.

A Holy Commonwealth. The kind of government that the seventeenth-century Puritans wanted, as their aims grew clear, was a theocracy: a Holy Commonwealth governed by God or God's representatives. The clergy were the representatives. They were men of vigorous intellect, deeply learned in theology, Hebrew and Greek. Church and state being closely united, the clergy guided the magistrates. Together they determined to see to it that the welfare of their Christian society was not to be subverted. They had given up much to come to America and they proposed to have and keep the sort of colony they wanted. Nonconformists in England, in Massachusetts they bristled at any suggestion of nonconformity to their rigid and angular conceptions. Quakers, for example, were banished and, if they returned, executed. Along with intolerance, however, the administration possessed qualities we can readily admire, such as willingness to accept an undesired office, a strong sense of justice and order, a remarkable probity of conduct. "I have found no record," says the historian Morison, "of malfeasance in public life in any New England colony or state, before the nineteenth century — there have been plenty since the religious sanction evaporated."

The Puritans came from the middle and lower classes. In the absence of an aristocracy such as England had, they accorded primacy to the wealthier and more cultivated merchants and landowners. Below them came the smaller merchants, storekeepers, farmers, artisans, mechanics, fishermen, free day laborers, and indentured servants and slaves (Indian slaves, a few Negroes). A fussy concern for social distinctions is well illustrated by the seating arrangements in church, which were based upon the class, age, and special qualifications of each person and upon the relative prestige of the seats themselves ("the fore seat in the front gallery shall be equal with the second seat in the body"). There was of course no leisure class; work, diligence, and thrift were regarded as godly virtues, as by middle-class Englishmen generally. They gave redoubled emphasis, in their frontier situation, to the view expressed, for example, by Richard Baxter in England: "If God show you a way in which you may lawfully get more than in another way (without wrong to your soul or any other), if you refuse this, and choose the less gainful way, you cross one of the ends of your calling, and you refuse to be God's steward." With the help of oxen and wooden plows they wrested wheat and Indian corn from the poor soil, but the economy depended increasingly upon lumbering, shipbuilding, fishing, and commerce. Particularly lucrative, they found, was the trade in rum and in slaves (Negroes were carried from Africa to the West Indies, later to the Southern plantations).

The Puritan Way of Life. Hearth and home counted heavily with the Puritans. The open fire on the enormous hearth served for both heating and cooking. A self-contained domestic economy required much labor, usually shared by an indentured servant or slave. Cows, hogs, and sheep were kept for food, leather, and wool, and the wool was carded, woven, and spun at home. Clothes were made at home. Fuel came from the woodlot or village commons. Candles were derived from tallow or bayberries. In the winter, time was devoted to making kitchen utensils, furniture, farm implements. As the children grew up (there were often ten or twelve, sometimes over twenty) all surviving members of the family co-operated to make it virtually self-sustaining.

Three words, it is said, were carved by a former occupant over the mantel of Nathaniel Ward's house in Ipswich, three words summing up the Puritan ethics: *Sobriety, Justice, Piety,* and to these Ward added a fourth — *Laughter.* We have come to realize that our conventional picture of the Puritans as grimly righteous and forbidding is scarcely adequate. Dour they often were — and often were not. They did not spend all their time avoiding pleasure and denying it to others.

Men of all classes and many women enjoyed the habit of smoking tobacco. According to Ward, whose liveliness led him to exaggerate, women "smoke in Bed, Smoke as they nead their Bread, Smoke whilst they're Cooking." The Puritans were anything but "Prohibitionists": both men and women found pleasure in beer, wine, and their favorite beverage, rum. Drunkenness was very common among all classes, in New England as in other colonies, and often reached scandalous proportions on such occasions as harvestings, funerals, college commencements, and the ordination of ministers. Dancing and card-playing, while generally frowned upon by the godly, had a place in New England even in the seventeenth century. It would be hard to say how much sex expression there was outside the marital union. At Plymouth, as Governor Bradford recorded, there was an outbreak of incontinence, "even sodomy and buggery." In the early eighteenth century fornication if eventually followed by marriage was looked upon, by all classes, as no serious sin or no sin at all. We also hear of "vile whoredoms."

Puritans had great interest in the arts of dress and the home. Even "the sternest of them," says James Truslow Adams, "had their portraits painted, wore rich clothes and accumulated beautiful furniture and costly plate." Dress closely corresponded to social position, and if common folk wore coarse and sober clothes, it was not from preference but in obedience to custom and law. In 1651 the General Court of Massachusetts proclaimed its "utter detestation that men and women of mean condition, education and calling, should take upon them the garbe of gentlemen by wearing of gold or silver lace, or buttons or pognots at their knees, or walke in great boots, or women of the same ranke to wear silke or tiffany hoods or scarfs." Gentlewomen tried to ape London fashions, sometimes importing dolls as models, and their wardrobes were resplendent with bright blue and scarlet silks, elaborate embroidery, and creamy lace. Wealthy men shared this taste for costly materials and vivid colors. Their frock coats were sometimes decorated with gold lace, and they wore knee breeches of brocade, plush, or silk, silk stockings, knee-buckles and shoe-buckles of silver or gold.

The artistic impulse of the people was combined with the practical. For example, utensils for the home were often carved into interesting forms and sometimes decorated with designs. The women dyed and wove bedspreads, varying colors and designs as fancy determined. Local ironsmiths designed and made hinges, door knockers, andirons, weathervanes and the like, with a grace and inventiveness that later times could envy. Silversmiths, in town and country, showed a taste comparable with that of the best craftsmen of Europe. Plainly, interest in the arts of the home was widespread in New England, as in the colonies to the south. It has even been possible for the twentieth-century historian to suggest that America was then more creatively artistic than it is now, even though there was no noteworthy achievement in the fine arts and *belles-lettres.* That the sense of beauty was so active among the Puritans is the more remarkable when we reflect that the currents of life ran strong at the two extremes — the practical and the religious. Concentrating on these, they had scant time or inclination to direct their creative imagination to the humanistic realm between the two extremes. Builders of a Christian commonwealth, they were absorbed in the tremendous task of subduing the wilderness without and the old Adam within.

If they did not produce great art and literature, the Puritans were nonetheless men of the Renaissance in their appreciation of Classical literature, despite the "pagan" or "heathen" nature of that literature. As Miller and Johnson remind us in their book *The Puritans,* the rich and powerful fusion of Puritanism and Hellenism achieved in England by Milton was "unique only in the grandeur of expression; the same combination of religious dogma and the classics, of Protestant theology and ancient morality, was the aim of the curriculum of Harvard College, and it was sustained, though on a rudimentary or pedestrian level, in the sermons of Yankee parsons throughout the seventeenth century." On the whole, it is anything but clear that the Puritans were "narrow," or at least that they were narrower than we (in our quite different way) or than men have been in most ages of history. Nor is it clear that they were less interested than we in "reality," though they had a different idea of reality, believed in it more earnestly, and would have thought ours superficial. And in the use of reason that supported their beliefs they showed an energy, a firmness, a continuity not surpassed, probably not equalled, by any later generation including our own. The last and greatest Puritan, Jonathan Edwards, had perhaps the finest intellect America has produced. Audiences followed with close attention carefully built argumentative sermons and even religious lectures five hours long! And if we, in our fluctuations of anxiety and zest, ask whether the Puritan belief made for happiness, Hooker in *The Soul's Exaltation* supplies an answer. Unbelievers remind him of persons struggling to pull a cart when it is off its wheels. They tug and toil, with scant success, and their lives are tedious to them. "But faith sets the cart upon the wheels, and carries all away easily and comfortably. . . . it is the most easiest life in all the world and hath the most delight in all the world."

GOD AS THE MEASURE

The early New Englanders did not use themselves as a measure of essential reality: they used God. Man they looked upon as not self-sufficient but wholly dependent. They were not rationalists, because they found human reason, unaided, an inadequate guide. They were not romanticists, because they deeply distrusted emotional desire and private intuition. They were not what *we* call realists, because they held ordinary, or matter-of-fact, or scientific reality to be something on the surface of life, not at its heart. Their psychology is a very old one, quite unlike the Freudian, behavioristic, and other interpretations of our time. The salient fact about human nature they held to be the soul, the image of God, individually created by God, infused into the body. In the great chain of being, man alone has the "rational soul," which contains the capacities of the lower forms of life, such as the senses and appetites, and adds to them the special human faculties, reason which guides and will which chooses.

In the Fall, man became entirely incapable of virtue save through the operation of divine grace. Owing to the corruption of his reason, of his will, of all his faculties, notably the imagination and the affections, man lay open to the perversions of sin. He could be restored to health only by the ministration of grace — "holy sparks of Heavenly fire" which might kindle him at any moment, inflame his higher nature, renew head and heart simultaneously. The sparks might come in various ways: an experience of bereavement, any affliction, any providential deliverance, but most commonly through the enkindling words of a minister of the Gospel. One can see how this might happen if the preacher were like John Cotton, a "living, breathing Bible" as he was described by the first graduate of Harvard. But so vital a presence was not necessary. "Whatsoever any faithful minister shall speak out of the Word," said Hooker, "that is also the voice of Christ."

The "Word" out of which the minister speaks is the Word of God, revealed in the Bible. In the Bible, God told man not all, but all that is needful for man to know. Beyond this declared will God has his secret will, not to be fathomed by his creatures; but his declared will, showing us our duties, is enough. We are to conceive of the Bible as a rule by which to measure ourselves and our essential knowledge and proper action, a rule superior to any that human experience might devise. "Crook not God's rules to the experience of men (which is fallible, and many times corrupt), but bring men unto the rule."

Open any of the typical books of the Puritans and you will come upon passages affirming that God or Providence, not erring man, is the final measure. Thus Urian Oakes, onetime president of Harvard: "The successes and events of undertakings and affairs are not determined infallibly by the greatest sufficiency of men, or second causes, but by the counsel and Providence of God ordering and governing time and chance according to his own good pleasure." Or: "See what a poor, dependent nothing-creature proud man is. . . . Man saith, he will do this and that: but he must ask God leave first. He saith, Today or tomorrow I will go to such a place, and buy and sell, and get gain; whereas he knows not what shall be." A merchant, soldier, scholar, or minister, however rationally he may strive, cannot prosper "unless God give him success." A good statesman aims at justice, but it must be the justice of one who fears God, "owns his commission to be from Him," "is a student in the law of God, and meditates in it day and night."

To the Puritans the Bible was a complete body of laws, bringing the spiritual life into relation not only with theology and ethics but all knowledge and all conduct. Anglicans and Puritans agreed in holding that scripture should be harmonious with human reason. To make this possible the Anglicans sought to reduce the doctrines required by scripture to a bare minimum, while the Puritans, extending scripture to cover the whole of life, undertook to show that the entire Bible, from beginning to end, is reasonable. In consequence of this literal and legalistic interpretation, scriptural evidence accompanied well-nigh everything that was written. Bible chapter-and-verse buttressed every proposition in books of theology, science, politics, morals, even had a place in poetry and love letters.

Calvinism. The Puritans claimed the right of the individual to read and interpret the Bible for himself. Yet in the fundamentals of their faith they usually found themselves in large agreement with the teachings of John Calvin, the French Protestant reformer of Geneva. The five points of Calvinism may be stated as follows: First, God elects individuals to be saved. Second, He designs complete redemption only for those elect. Third, fallen man is himself incapable of true faith and repentance. Fourth, God's grace is sufficient for the salvation of the elect. Fifth, a soul once regenerated is never ultimately lost. When the Puritans of New England agreed with Calvin, they did so not because Calvin was authoritative for them but because his teachings seemed confirmed by the Bible and experience.

The Puritan faith made life anything but dull. It produced a high excitement. The world was the setting for a great drama, the drama of man in relation to God and Satan, to Heaven and Hell. It was the drama of the individual human soul, facing unspeakable bliss or unspeakable torment. It was also the drama of the Christian society. Having come to America as a promised land, the Puritans thought of themselves as a chosen people. In the Holy Commonwealth, the Bible was the constitution, only church members were citizens, and God's ministers guided the state. The more this corporate blessedness was subverted by Satan — acting through the Indians, the witches, and the internal conflicts of the churches — the more passionately was it believed in and propagated. But not even such strenuous leaders as Increase and Cotton Mather could halt the forces of disintegration, and in the failure of Jonathan Edwards and the Great Awakening the whole Calvinistic structure was finally doomed. It was not disproved; it was merely abandoned.

All along, Calvinism had met with opposition of various sorts. In the early years it was shaken by antinomianism, till Anne Hutchinson was banished for sundry heresies, among them the doctrine that God reveals himself directly to individual persons, which ran counter to the Calvinist teaching that God's final revelation was the Bible. Another heresy was the doctrine of Arminianism that salvation could depend on "good works," that is, moral living, which was rejected by the orthodox on the ground that it diminished God's sovereignty — made man a bit uppish. In these and other dissenting opinions we can now see that the age was moving, however gradually, away from the concept of a strictly God-centered world toward the man-centered world of the eighteenth century. It was moving from dependence of man on God to dependence of man on himself, from humility toward Providence to pride in human powers. For a new age was coming on, with new beliefs and interests, almost the opposite of Puritan orthodoxy. A rising secular spirit was assuming or proclaiming that the proper study of mankind is man, that man is not inherently evil but naturally good, and that he is not an exile awaiting the time of felicity (or damnation) but a reasonable creature engaged in the pursuit of happiness in this pleasant world.

Today, we feel less comfortable in the Puritan age than in the age of reason that followed, less at home with Winthrop and Cotton Mather than with Franklin and Jefferson. And yet — the scholarly editors of *The Puritans* conclude — "we are terribly aware once more, thanks to the revelation of psychologists and the events of recent political history, that men are not perfect or essentially good. The Puritan description of them, we have been reluctantly compelled to admit, is closer to what we have witnessed than the description given in Jeffersonian democracy or in transcendentalism."

PURITAN LITERATURE

Settlers of the Atlantic frontier, builders of commonwealths, men of morals and religion, the Puritans were otherwise absorbed than in the production of *belles-lettres*. Yet they did write a considerable amount of prose, much more than the colonists to the south, and more verse than one would expect. We would find it interesting to follow the course of their writings chronologically, from Bradford's journal on the Pilgrim settlement to Jonathan Edwards' defense of Calvinism in the increasingly alien eighteenth century — he died in the year when Franklin published "The Way to Wealth." But here, instead of proceeding in the order of time, let us glance at the literature with reference to the types or forms commonly used. They were: historical writings, sermons, and poetry.

Historical Writings. Historical writings were motivated by a desire to record what had happened or was happening in a very "New" England. Often they consisted of little more than chronicles or annals, setting down contemporary events as Bradford did for the Plymouth plantation and Winthrop for Massachusetts Bay. The scope of other historical works may be suggested by a few titles: Nathaniel Morton's *New England's Memorial,* William Woods' *New England's Prospect* (its natural features), Edward Johnson's *History of New England* (covering 1628-1652), William Hubbard's *Narrative of the Troubles with the Indians in New England,* and the most famous historical work of the period, Cotton Mather's *Magnalia Christi Americana, or The Ecclesiastical History of New England* (covering 1620-1698).

It goes without saying that such books do not illustrate our modern attempt to write objective or scientific history. The New Englanders generally wrote what may be called providential history. That is, they interpreted their matter in the light of the theory that the key to history is Providence, the direct divine guidance of the world. Following a tradition that goes back to St. Augustine and classical antiquity, they believed that the great, commanding reality in life is the operation of God's will, in general and in detail. The art of history, consequently, must show this through things that have happened, must bring out the high meaning of particular events and the general sequence of events.

Along with history there were other forms of narrative record. Thus, within the loose structure of his ecclesiastical history of

New England, Cotton Mather included a large number of biographies. The Puritans also wrote autobiographies, such as the "Personal Narrative" of Jonathan Edwards, and no end of diaries. Practically all Puritans who could write kept a diary, as a record of constant self-examination. The center of concern was the course not of the outer life, but of the inner. Every fluctuation of inner condition, every temptation, doubt, bewilderment, struggle, every moment of insight or ecstacy, of deep humility or resurgence of pride (if only pride in being humble) was of absorbing interest to men and women uncertain whether their hearts had indeed been visited by grace, whether they were truly progressing in their pilgrimage toward the Celestial City.

Diarists had little or nothing to say of their mundane affairs, their vocations, their practical decisions, how people dealt with each other, behaved, dressed, etc. To this there is one notable exception, a late Puritan, Samuel Sewall. His life span carried him from the middle of the seventeenth century through the first third of the eighteenth, and his diary reflects the spirit of the changing times. The earlier entries record the usual self-examination, but as time went on this Yankee judge found it worth while to set down more and more details of a worldly sort, with a sense of the picturesque and a personal flavor that give his pages what we like to call "human interest."

Sermons. Most of the published prose of the Puritan age consisted of sermons and controversial writings. These were central in the intellectual life which the clergy controlled. In our own time the map of life is drawn for us by scientists, journalists, novelists, by the producers of motion pictures and television, but in Puritan New England it was virtually the clergy alone who performed this function. In addition to providing leadership in church and state, they were the writing class. Various aspects of church and state, of theology and church government, or moral and practical needs in a Christian society were subjects of many treatises and tracts. They were written by such men as Roger Williams, Nathaniel Ward, John Cotton, Thomas Hooker, Increase Mather, Cotton Mather, and later, at their best, by Jonathan Edwards. These ministers and scores of others also published numerous sermons.

Sermons, in fact, may be taken as the typical form of Puritan literature. To most people today, seventeenth century sermons might seem alien and unmeaning, but to the congregations who heard or read them they were often absorbingly important, given close attention, discussed, reconsidered. They provided spiritual enlightenment by means of intellectual stimulation. A sermon was an argument built like a lawyer's brief, with major divisions, headings, and subheadings. After the elucidation of the text came a direct, dry statement of the "Doctrine." Then came the demonstration or proof, in which the reasons and often the sub-reasons were numbered 1, 2, 3, etc. The points were given a logical order, but without transition between them. Doctrine was followed by "Use" or application, again in 1, 2, 3 fashion. There was no peroration or climactic oratory; the sermon simply ended when the argument was complete.

Thus the Puritan sermon was addressed primarily to the logical faculty. It was intended to convince the reason, not excite the imagination; to instruct the mind, not stir the passions. It was quite different from the rich, harmonious oratory of Anglican pulpits in the mother country. The general effect aimed at was called "plainness." Thomas Hooker, perhaps the greatest of New England preachers, said, "I have accounted it the chiefest part of judicious learning to make a hard point easy and familiar in explication." The language was to be fit, not fancy, for "fitness of words," as another writer conceived, "puts wheels to the chariots to carry them to the mind." If (as here) a metaphor or simile was used, it was not to adorn the homespun of the discourse or to divert or dazzle the listener, but simply to make the teaching clear or vital. Often we find abstractions made concrete by means of homely images drawn from farming, fishing, village life, and other familiar concerns. Only rarely do we come upon a passage where language and rhythm are finely molded by poetic feeling. Such a passage occurs in an election day sermon by William Hubbard in 1676. The divine principle of Order he finds in the goodly fabric of our world, and in the invisible heavens where the Almighty has reared his mansion place, and, between the two, in the skies within our ken:

> . . . the firmament, the pavement of that glorious mansion place, although it be the roof of this lower world, may we not there see one star differing from another in glory? There is placed the Sun, the lord and ruler of the day, as well as the Moon, that rules the night, together

with the stars, as the common-people of that upper region,
who yet do immediately veil their glory, and withdraw
their light, when their bridegroom cometh forth of his
chamber.

The poet Coleridge would have enjoyed this, if we may judge
from his own famous sentence about the moon and the stars in
the prose gloss to "The Ancient Mariner."

Poetry. The Puritans published little poetry: a very few
books of verse, the rest dispersed in almanacs, biographies, funeral sermons, etc. This was not because they wrote little, for they
wrote much; but most of what they wrote was circulated in manu-
script or simply preserved in private or not even preserved. What
does this mean?

It cannot be that they who wrote so much were hostile to
poetry. Heirs of the Renaissance, the Puritans valued the ancient
classics, esteemed such moderns as Spencer, Sidney, and (later)
Milton, and of course were in sympathy with the Renaissance
belief in the ethical foundation of poetry. With such a tradition
behind them, and living intensely in the present, they had, it
would seem, a situation favorable to a high order of religious poetry. For their failure to publish a body of epic and lyric poetry we
must look for reasons other than hostility. One has already been
suggested: they were too absorbed in the practical demands of
settlement. At the same time they were too absorbed in an austere
religion, which made them fearful of the dangers latent in the
senses and passions that poetry cultivates; also, in their zeal for
solid substance of thought, they undervalued aesthetic expression.
Again, they had no public familiar with literary art to address
themselves to, and, as likely as not, they simply had a deficiency
of talent.

Certainly they made an ominous beginning! In the *Bay Psalm
Book* three ministers joined in a literal translation of the Psalms,
not even intended to be "poetry" but rather material to be adjusted
to the tunes sung in the churches. Two lines will suffice to show
the dreadful result:

> The Lord to me a shepherd is,
> want therefore shall not I.

The subordination of aesthetic quality to sound doctrine is
strikingly shown by the "best-seller" of Puritan verse, Wiggles-

worth's *Day of Doom*. It is not devoid of poetic power, but on
the whole is little more than versified Calvinism which the pious
could readily learn by heart. Within a hundred years it went
through ten editions. There is vastly more merit in the work of
Anne Bradstreet. Though she was given to imitating an unfor-
tunate model, she had an effectively simple way of her own. We
can see that she was capable of a free genuine expression, though
she refrained from going beyond the limits set by decorum. But
the one poet who plainly emerges above the rest of the Puritans
is Edward Taylor, who published only a little but left in manu-
script a large collection of verse virtually unknown till the
twentieth century. He is our seventeenth-century "Metaphysical,"
reminiscent of Donne, Crashaw, and other English poets of the
time. Here for once Puritan religious poetry showed that it could
not only be devout in its orthodox substance, but vigorous, passionate, sometimes ecstatic, in its expression. The language is
fresh and tense, fusing thought and feeling. Most surprising are
passages where the imagery attains a frank, sensuous warmth
which, as Kenneth Murdock suggests, might well have seemed
to many Puritans dangerous, a warmth more to be expected in an
Anglican than in a Puritan poet:

> My lovely one, I fain would love thee much,
>   But all my love is none at all I see;
> Oh! let thy beauty give a glorious touch
>   Upon my heart, and melt to love all me.
> Lord, melt me all up into love for thee,
>   Whose loveliness excells what love can be.

GENTLEMEN OF VIRGINIA

The English colonies differed widely. Next door to intolerant
Massachusetts was a colony dedicated to complete religious
liberty, a colony which Cotton Mather of Boston derided by saying that, if any man lost his religion, he could be sure to find it
in Rhode Island. A little farther south were the Dutch, French,
and English of New Netherland, which became New York. Then
there was the "sylvania" of Penn, the English Quaker, an exception to the rule of shameless aggression against the Indians. His
colony, before the Revolution, was about one-third German.
Again to the south was one founded by an English Catholic,
Lord Baltimore, a colony which before long had an established

church — Anglican. Then Anglican Virginia, so unlike Puritan New England and so important in American civilization that we shall do well to take a look at it and its leaders.

In the moist heat of Virginia, "Tobacco only was the business," observed a contemporary, "and for aught that I could hear every man madded upon that and little thought or looked for anything else." Fortunes were made in a single year. The crop was cultivated increasingly by Negro slaves, and by the end of the colonial period the population was half black. Instead of the small farms and villages and towns of New England, Virginia had spacious plantations and a widely scattered population. Its society was made up of slaves and servants, yeomen or small farmers, and a minority of great planters who gained social and political control.

The Planting Aristocracy. From the beginning the great planters constituted an aristocracy. Only a few were aristocratic in their origins; the rest, having or acquiring capital, made their way to the top by building up large estates — a foundation for social status, power, and prerogatives. By 1725 Virginia had a society based on slavery and was more or less feudal. The arrogance of the tight little aristocracy was offset by its recognition of public service as a duty, by its obligation to provide a sound example to those lower in the scale, and by its desire to maintain the Renaissance tradition of the gentleman, characterized by such virtues as fortitude, prudence, temperance, justice, liberality, courtesy. One can see how a leadership of this sort, later invaluable in the service of state and nation, was bred by the plantation way of life. A boy brought up on an estate of several thousand acres took part, from an early age, in directing the work of perhaps two score or more slaves and servants. He was trained to duties concerning the growing of tobacco, the care of orchards, the raising of livestock, the transaction of business with English importers. Through association with his father and with visitors who came to the plantation he must have learned much about the processes and personalities in the colony's politics. It was a mode of life, as the historian Wertenbaker says, that encouraged him to be "practical, inquiring, robust, and self-reliant, even though it seldom instilled into him the inventive spirit or inspired him to literary effort."

Gentlemen planters assumed leadership not only in civil and

military affairs but even in religion. Orthodox Anglicans, they controlled the Church, which they regarded as an essential part of a sound commonwealth, a means toward decent living. Decent living they found compatible with a good deal of worldliness. They sought riches and loved the luxuries that riches bring, fine houses, fashionable furniture, Oriental rugs and tapestries, abundance of pewter and silver plate, jewels, clothes in the mode. Dancing was the most popular social diversion. They did a vast amount of drinking, but as a rule drank like gentlemen. Favored pastimes included not only hunting and fishing, but horse racing, cockfighting, and cardplaying, with gambling on the side. Yet the claims of religion were always in the background. In *The First Gentlemen of Virginia,* Louis B. Wright notes that "many a planter conscientiously held prayers for his household and acted as the spiritual as well as the secular head of his little community. Rarely were even hard-drinking, hard-swearing, slave-driving plantation masters without a reverence for religion." Remembering this, we shall not be surprised that the Virginia House of Burgesses, the first legislature that met on American soil, enacted that "All persons whatsoever upon the Sabbath days shall frequent divine service and sermons, both forenoon and afternoon."

William Byrd of Westover. In early Southern literature we would, however, look in vain for the sermons, religious treatises, and diaries of the inner life that were characteristic of New England. Nor could we find poets equivalent to Mrs. Bradstreet and Edward Taylor. The writings that have come down to us are in the main descriptive and historical. Thus, George Alsop wrote a vigorous description, *A Character of the Province of Maryland,* and Robert Beverley, landed gentleman of Virginia, wrote *The History and Present State of Virginia,* showing a good capacity for observation and occasional satire. But the most interesting and important Southern writer was another Virginian, William Byrd the younger, the author of *A Progress to the Mines, A Journey to the Land of Eden,* and *The History of the Dividing Line.* The last is an account of a surveying trip to fix the boundary between Virginia and North Carolina, the other two describe journeys to examine some of the author's vast land holdings. He had inherited 26,231 acres from his father, William Byrd the elder, a merchant who had established the family fortune by dealing in tobacco, trading with the Indians, and importing slaves and rum.

At the time of his father's death Byrd was in England, where he had been a number of years engaged in business, in law training, and in gay living, and where he was to spend more years later. An accomplished gentleman, he moved freely in fashionable English society. Devoted to the London theater, he knew the Restoration dramatists, William Congreve, Nicholas Rowe, and, intimately, William Wycherley. From his English associations he naturally assimilated interests and attitudes, as well as something of the shape and flavor of contemporaneous writing. Back in Virginia, Byrd lived at Westover, on the James, a house which he inherited and rebuilt handsomely in brick and filled with beautiful furniture, fine glass, and silver imported from England, along with other things befitting his station — including portraits of English nobility whom he had known and with whom he corresponded. To one of them, the Earl of Orrery, he wrote a description of his life as a planter:

> I have a large family of my own, and my doors are open to everybody, yet I have no bills to pay, and half a crown will rest undisturbed in my pocket for many moons together. Like one of the patriarchs, I have my flocks and my herds, my bondmen and bondwomen, and every sort of trade amongst my own servants, so that I live in a kind of independence of everyone but Providence. However, this sort of life is without expense, yet it is attended with a great deal of trouble. I must take care to keep all my people to their duty, to set all the springs in motion, and to make everyone draw his equal share to carry the machine forward. But then 'tis an amusement in this silent country.

This broad picture we may fill in with the varied details of his daily living as recorded in a very personal diary that came to light only in 1939. Here, like Pepys, he set down in shorthand the intimate events, the tasks and amusements, that made up his days. This account is the more valuable to us in that the colonists of the South, unlike the New Englanders, very rarely kept diaries.

An eager collector of books, Byrd built up a library of over 3,600 titles, the largest in Virginia, equalled only, in other colonies, by Cotton Mather's in Massachusetts. A remarkably balanced library, it included history, biography, and travels (more than

250 works); books of law, medicine, and divinity (around 150 each); books of science, mathematics, architecture, painting, philosophy, agriculture, distillery, cooking, etc.; Greek and Latin authors in the original languages (nearly 300); works in French (over 200); English literature, especially the Elizabethan and Restoration dramatists. As a busy and active man, he could not have read all the books he owned, but he did have considerable intellectual curiosity, and he did read Greek and Hebrew before breakfast!

By the time of his death Byrd had increased his ownership of land to more than 179,000 acres. He enjoyed the goods of the world in abundance, but with a sense of responsibility to his class, to the province of Virginia which he loved, and to the Christian standards of his heritage. Like other gentlemen planters, he held religion in high respect. Yet he was certainly without the "agonized conscience" of the Calvinists of New England or the spiritual quietude of the Quakers of the middle colonies. We shall not be far wrong in thinking of him as dominantly a blend of gay gentility and worldly rationalism.

"Worldly rationalism" already takes us into a new period, the Age of Reason. By the time of Byrd's death in 1744, men could look back to the period of settlement in an age of religion, and forward to a period of material prosperity in an age of politics. Had they been able to see the future more definitely, they would have known, that within about three decades the colonies were to declare their independence, that a Virginia gentleman would lead their feeble armies toward final victory, and another Virginia gentleman lead the attack on aristocracy in favor of government of the people, by the people, and for the people.

THE NEO–CLASSIC AGE

Human Reason and Natural Order

"*All, nature made, in reason's sight
Is order all and all is right.*"
— Freneau

In the eighteenth century the faith of the Puritans subsided. Jonathan Edwards, it is true, carried it far into the century — made a last great stand in defense of a lost cause. But the world in which he lived had already turned to new interests, adopted a new outlook on life. Broadly speaking the eighteenth century was dedicated not to religion but to science and politics. Its leaders were no longer Christian ministers like Mather and Edwards but natural philosophers like Franklin and Jefferson. The change

20

was profound; in many respects the old and the new were opposite. Otherworldliness gave way to worldliness. A divine, a God-centered world became a human, a man-centered world. Life guided by the Holy Bible became life guided by human reason. No longer was the world a place where Providence, ever present and ever active, controlled everything that happened, even trivial events. To the eye of reason the world was now part of a machine universe which, once set in motion, had run of its own accord ever since. God himself, no longer a person, a father to be loved and feared, became a remote and impersonal intelligence, a "First Cause" that started the machine and left it to operate in perfect order according to mathematical and physical laws. And Jesus, Son of God, became Jesus, son of man.

The proper study of mankind was no longer God but man. Man had been a spiritual being in fleshly form, but now, according to a new psychology, he must be thought of as coming into the world devoid of ideas and moral principles, as if he were a blank piece of paper to be written on by sense experience. In place of the old view that just a few souls are "elect," chosen for salvation in eternity, came the view that all men are entitled to share in the "pursuit of happiness" in their own time. Government by an aristocracy of birth and wealth was beginning to be altered by emphasis on leadership by those naturally best, regardless of class — a leadership subject to the consent of the governed. The evils of civilization were now explained, not by the old doctrine of original sin (Adam's fall) but by the effect of an unsound social environment. The relief of man's estate might be expected to come not so much from religion as from science, education, and politics, by which the environment could be improved.

It goes without saying that these contrasts have been too sharply drawn. The difference between two ages is always complex. We know how highly the Puritans esteemed human reason, and science as well. And we must bear in mind that, while the new outlook was common in the intellectual class that set the tone for the new age, the great majority of the population was ready to accept only certain features of the new order. A large number of people, in fact, clung to old beliefs and values with hardly any change.

So long as we remember that all periods are complex, particularly to those living in them, we may sensibly choose a unifying name to apply to the period we are now concerned with. In point of time it was, roughly, the *Eighteenth Century*. In politics, it was the *Revolutionary Period*. In terms of ideas, attitudes, values, it was the *Age of Reason*. In relation to literary art, the subject of our study, it was the *Neo-Classic Age*. This age, in turning away from the Puritan view of life, gave primary allegiance to that Classical culture which for the Puritans had been secondary. For much that it valued most, it found its best examples in the humanistic world of the Greeks, man-centered and rational, and in the civilization of the Romans, with their sense of law, order, and dignity.

REASON AS THE MEASURE

How did it come about that faith in human reason gradually suppressed the beliefs and exaltations of the Puritan Age? Why did men give up their hard-won sureness and security? Why were the men and women of the new age so different from John and Margaret Winthrop ("Our God . . . will be our God to the end, to carry us along through this course of our pilgrimage") or from Jonathan and Sarah Edwards ("sweetly conversing with Christ, and wrapt and swallowed up in God")? What did mere reason — cold reason that chills the heart — have to offer that was so attractive?

Rationalism, developing in Europe, looked not to the Bible but to the realm of nature. Nature, said Galileo (1564-1642), can be known only by one who understands her language — the language of mathematics. A little later Descartes, French founder of modern philosophy, affirmed that mathematical knowledge might become the source of all other knowledge, and conceived that the entire world of matter, including animal life (and even man. except for his power of reason) is determined by the laws of physics. The universe as a whole is simply a stupendous machine. Then Descartes' sketch of a machine universe was filled out scientifically by Isaac Newton in one of the most influential books of the world, the *Principia Mathematica* (1687). He proved to a fascinated generation that the falling apple and the stars in their courses obey the same laws of gravitation and motion. The order of nature is apparently a mathematical harmony, its laws uniform, fixed, undeviating. The universe is a perpetual motion machine, self-regulating, operating in time and space.

To us in the twentieth century, dominated by concepts of evolutionary change and relativity, this mathematical vision of a fixed mechanical order of things has lost its power of enchantment. But to the educated public of the Age of Reason the work of Newton became a new Bible. Its dazzling reception is suggested by the lines of Alexander Pope:

> Nature and Nature's laws lay hid in night:
> God said, *Let Newton be!* and all was light.

To explain such a response we must look into the inferences that thinking men drew. A generation weary of religious conflict and political disorder, they needed blueprints for a sane and solid reconstruction, such as Newton seemed to offer. Gladly they embraced a new faith. They believed that the clear light of truth was no longer to be blurred by the chaotic, the abnormal, the irrational. Nature itself is rational and orderly throughout. Perfection comes from perfection: the exquisite order of the universe must be the masterpiece of God, the supreme artist. Natural law is held to be the authoritative word of God. Nature — Reason — Science: these were now almost interchangeable with each other and with God. Surely for man, as a part of the "stupendous whole," here was an idea worthy of trust. We need only seek, it seems, in all fields of thought and life, that which is *natural,* that which is *reasonable,* that which is in harmony with *science* (clear and distinct demonstration) and with *God* (the First Cause of all subsequent causes and effects).

To do this we must cast aside all traditions that are blind, irrational, superstitious, fanatical. We are not to be sparing in our criticism of the traditions of Christianity, or of absolute monarchy, or whatever else has been handed down to us. For such criticism we have some helpful standards. Since the laws of science are uniform, we are to look for the *universal,* i.e. ideals and customs always and everywhere the same, despite superficial variety. For example, we should consider the Orient as well as our Western world, to determine what they have in common. What is national may be mere prejudice; our view should be cosmopolitan. We are also to look to the *primitive,* not as an "escape" to indulge our emotions, but as that stage of society, whether actual or theoretical, in which things are still rational, not yet twisted out of shape by human error or refined almost past recognition. The clear simplicities of that early time have a validity self-evident to our minds. By faithful reasoning from axiomatic truths we can assure an enlightenment and happiness that man has never known. Let us drop the partial and see the whole; let us abandon the artificial and return to the natural and rational; let us penetrate to the very nature of things! As Tom Paine made bold to declare, the Creation itself is "the Word of God," and science is the medium by which "man can see God, as it were, face to face."

This is a religious affirmation, It goes far beyond the starting point, the mathematics and physics of Newton, and well beyond a mere trust in reason. Many of the intellectuals most remote from Orthodox Christianity were religious, in an eighteenth century way, believing in what was called natural religion or deism.

Deism. Natural religion, as opposed to revealed religion, denied the authority of any religious beliefs not held everywhere, in all times, by all men. Thus, it could not admit the divinity of Christ or the doctrine of the Trinity. When all such doctrines had been rejected, what remained? What doctrines could unaided human reason establish as universally valid? What beliefs are agreeable to nature and science? They might be stated as follows: First, there is an all-powerful God. Second, man is required to live virtuously. Third, in a future life the virtuous will be rewarded, the wicked punished. This simple creed was acceptable to deists and orthodox Christians alike. The orthodox could subscribe to natural religion while claiming that revealed religion was necessary to complete it; deists could subscribe to it as sufficient by itself. Both in England and America deism appealed strongly to the more intellectual classes. In America it represented in varying degrees the view of men like Franklin, Washington, Jefferson, Ethan Allen, Paine, Freneau. Radical deists like Paine harshly attacked the most cherished beliefs of the orthodox; the orthodox sometimes countered by condemning deism as outright atheism.

It was not atheism, because it provided for a God — of a sort. God was to be put in his place — outside the range of human experience, outside our world; absent from, not present within us and the world. God was the creative mind that designed the universe and set the machine going with a stock of laws assuring order, but thereafter not meddling in the world's affairs, nor concerning himself more for man than for his other creations. This First Cause of all things is discoverable, by human reason, through the rational processes of nature. In ruling God out of the world, thoroughgoing deists of course threw out all the divine interference through the miraculous and the providential, but others sometimes used the idea of Providence at least occasionally. And there were even those, like Shaftesbury and Pope, who, despite their deistic views, inconsistently brought God back into the world, as in Pope's familiar lines:

> All are but parts of one stupendous whole,
> Whose body is Nature, and God the soul.

A concept like this helped to prepare the way for romanticism, for the "Presences of Nature" worshipped by Wordsworth and by Emerson and Thoreau after him. But the concept is clearly contrary to the mechanical interpretation of the universe that is a usual mark of deism.

As for man, deism employed the view of human nature worked out by the philosophical school of Locke. We have already touched upon the sober theory of John Locke that man's experience through the five senses is basic, that his response to sensory stimuli causes him to form simple ideas, these in turn building up in his mind into more and more complex ideas, so that all that we know really goes back to the senses. Evidently men do not come into the world predestined by a class-conscious God who provides one way for the elect and another way for the masses. Nor is it the nature of man to come into the world with a mind already stocked with ideas, latent ideas that become plain with experience. To use Locke's term, there are no "innate ideas." The mind at birth is simply a blank. Everything written on it comes later. And the writing is done by environment, by the institutions and customs of the state, the church, the school, the economic system, etc. If these were sound and rational, the results would be good.

Increasingly associated with the religion of reason was a belief in progress (not to be confused with our idea of organic evolution). Belief in progress had grown out of the new science, of which Bacon was the prophet and Newton the Messiah. With justified pride, many men came to feel that there would be endless progress in scientific knowledge and material conveniences. From this they passed on to a more questionable belief in social progress. Could not a new social science improve the environment by changing the institutions, above all education, and soon bring on a society enlightened, wise, and prosperous? In this way was not man perfectible? We should not look backward but forward. The Golden Age lies not in the ancient past but in the future. There can be, there will be, a Heaven on earth! Such was the faith of many intellectuals in England, and in America as well. Typically, an American named Chipman affirmed that man is nothing less than "a being capable of improvement, in a progression of which he knows not the limits." Faith in progress blended easily with the optimism of a frontier land of opportunity, and in the nineteenth century was to receive fresh impetus through the idea of evolution.

The religion of reason was strongly opposed. While it was spreading, from the second decade to the end of the eighteenth century, the two leading orthodox churches — the Congregational (Calvinist) and the Anglican — were well entrenched, though weakening by deist infiltration and attrition. A more formidable opponent was the counter-offensive of the Revivalist movement. Religious feeling revolted against worldliness and skepticism. In contrast to the serene common sense of Franklin and the acid rationalism of Paine, we must place the emotional explosions of revivals, with their visions and trances, their weeping and swooning. They occurred from Massachusetts to Georgia, and by 1800 crossed the mountains into Kentucky and Tennessee. They throve especially among the lower classes and at the frontier. In the early nineteenth century, Methodists, Baptists, Presbyterians, and others had assured the establishment of Protestant evangelism as the dominant religion of America. Even the colleges changed, almost suddenly. According to Lyman Beecher, who entered Yale in 1793, "The college was in a most ungodly state. The college church was almost extinct. Most of the students were skeptical, and rowdies were plenty. Wine and liquors were kept in many rooms; intemperance, profanity, gambling, and licentiousness were common. I hardly know how I escaped. . . . That was the day of the infidelity of the Tom Paine school." But in 1802, Benjamin Silliman, then a Yale tutor, converted in the great revival of that year, was able to write to his mother: "It would delight your heart, my dear mother, to see how the trophies of the Cross are multiplied in this institution. Yale College is a little temple: prayer and praise seem to be the delight of the greater part of the students, while those who are still unfeeling are awed into respectful silence."

While the religion of reason was still thriving, it was strongest in the cities — especially Philadelphia, where colonial culture attained its fullest expression.

The Worldly Charm of Philadelphia

The congenial home city of the reasonable Mr. Franklin became the largest and most illustrious in the colonies. Its population of 40,000 made it, at the beginning of the Revolution, the second largest city in the British Empire. And London and Paris themselves, in the eyes of Thomas Jefferson in 1786, were "not so handsome as Philadelphia." The most worldly city on the American continent, it was notable for its wealth, its tolerance and moderation, its practical and cultural attainments, its scientific and cosmopolitan spirit.

Philadelphia seemed destined for prosperity. Its people were intelligent and industrious, its natural advantages outstanding. From the finest agricultural region in the colonies, meat, lumber and crops flowed like a tide. At its wharves commerce and prosperity increased as shipping moved up and down the Atlantic coast and to the West Indies and Europe. Wholesalers, exporters, importers, often land speculators, its merchants rather easily grew rich. At first they were mostly Quakers, later Anglicans.

Social Groups. The earlier Quakers, in the City of Brotherly Love or elsewhere, contributed to American life a tradition of plain living, of singularly pure religious inwardness, of charity firmly based on Christian love — qualities already familiar to us through the journal of John Woolman. The more conservative Friends in Philadelphia clung to the old simple ways, frowning upon the luxury and ostentation they saw increasing on all sides. Many others, acquiring riches, acquired also the love of riches and rich living, till it was hard to distinguish them from wealthy non-Quakers. Not a few broke away from their Society and joined the fashionable Anglicans. John Adams, coming from Boston at the time of the Revolution, remarked upon Quakers hovering, so to speak, between old and new style: still garbed in broad-brimmed hats and using the familiar "thee" instead of "you," but living in handsome brick mansions filled with modish furniture and brilliant silver. Meanwhile the number of Quakers had declined from a fourth of the population in 1750 to a seventh in 1770, while the Presbyterian and Anglican population increased.

Anglican and Quaker merchants ably controlled the commercial, political, social, and cultural life of the city. Like the successful planters of Virginia, they became an aristocracy, on the whole admirable, though certainly capable of arrogance. There were old Tory ladies in whose eyes, we may well infer, Franklin had made his first error (*erratum*) in permitting himself to be born of a mere candle-maker. They never forgave him, even when he became a man of wealth and one of the most highly civilized persons of his time on either side of the Atlantic.

Beneath the merchant grandees were the prosperous middle-class shopkeepers, craftsmen, mariners, farmers, etc., also men of leisure interested in scholarship and science. In this period of the rising middle class, admission to it from the humbler ranks was nowhere freer than in Philadelphia. Of the many aspects of its life we can form a picture through the autobiography of that middle-class genius, Ben Franklin. Partly middle class, mainly lower in the scale, were the Germans, who contributed to the moral solidity of the city and to its skills and crafts. German was displayed on signboards over shops, spoken in the streets, read in a newspaper such as *Der Wöchentliche Philadelphische Staatsbote*. Franklin was far from alone in his fear that German culture might dominate the entire colony and erase the English language.

Early in the century, when the town was small, there was no great difference between richer and poorer, so that an observer could report in 1724: "There are people who have been living here for forty years and have not seen a beggar in Philadelphia." Later the townspeople were disturbed by the "poor from foreign parts." Long the chief colonial port of entry for immigrants, Philadelphia had to make temporary provisions for large numbers of Germans and Scotch-Irish before they moved on to the farms or frontier. At the same time the gap between its own rich and poor citizens increased, and class lines tightened.

The pride of life in the upper classes was shown by their dress. The middle decades of the century, according to C. M. Andrews, "represent in the history of this country the highest point reached in richness of costume, variety of color, peculiarities of decoration, and excess of frills and furbelows on the part of both sexes." Men of fashion could adorn themselves in dainty blue or resplendent scarlet, with lacy cuffs hanging over the hand, while ladies extended themselves with high headdresses, and hoop skirts wide one way but not the other, so that on coming to a door they had to enter sideways. The gentry enjoyed dancing — the gracious, decorous minuet. Gentlemen in pink coats rode to hounds. Popular amusements were bowling on the green, cockfighting, bullbaiting. All classes played cards for stakes. All classes frequented taverns, for serious discussion, idle chatter, quarreling, drinking and drunkenness, according to the individual preference and the type of place chosen. In the lusty life of the eighteenth century sex relations were often relaxed, but people in general held to rather strict standards. Crime was not serious enough to impress us, in our more violent time.

Cultural Life. The cultural life of the city we may approach through the salons, where celebrities enjoyed the social art of conversation. There were Quaker salons, such as that of Mrs. George Logan, which brought together men like Washington, Jefferson, John Randolph of Roanoke, Genêt, Kosciusko, Dupont de Nemours. In the Anglican set there was, for instance, Elizabeth Graeme, daughter of the leading physician, hostess for Saturday evenings so intelligently animated that Dr. Benjamin Rush called them Athenian. She attracted all the scientific and literary leaders of the city, and men of distinction from all the colonies. In the view of Bayard, French author of a travel book, American ladies "would have been considered remarkable even at the brilliant and witty French court."

Outwardly, Philadelphia was impressive because of its achievements in architecture. It had the finest church building in all the colonies: Christ Church, stately and ornate, with a London organ. An Anglican place of worship, it was attended by persons of wealth, fashion, and position. The city also had the largest public building in colonial America — the State House of the Pennsylvania capital, with a grand staircase and rich carvings. There were scores of beautiful mansions in the city. And in the countryside landscape architecture had free play. At the residence of William Peters, for example, the great hall served as a pivot for the formal gardens, which included a vista terminated by an obelisk, a labyrinth of cedar and spruce hedge, a Chinese temple, and statues of Apollo, Diana, Mercury, and Fame.

Fine cabinetmakers adorned the interior of residences with elegant Chippendale tables, highboys, etc., and, as styles changed, with Marlborough, Sheraton, and Hepplewhite furniture. Silversmiths provided delicately graceful candlesticks, tea and coffee services — and the inkstand used at the signing of the Declaration and the Constitution. There were portrait painters, such as Gustavus Hesselius, whose canvases decorated the homes of wealthy merchants, but Philadelphia lost its best artist, Benjamin West, to England, where he succeeded Sir Joshua Reynolds as president of the Royal Academy.

More interesting than any of these arts, to Dr. Franklin as civic leader, were such cultural concerns as libraries, bookstores, education, and the advancement of science. Franklin's discussion group, the Junto, led to the formation of the Library Company, a group of twenty-four, soon a hundred subscribers. They imported work in such fields as history, literature, philosophy, and science, and were presently permitted to keep their collection in the State House. By the middle of the century there were also the Library of Friends and that of the American Philosophical Society. Bookshops were started, six by the middle of the century. Andrew Bradford specialized in religious books, but Franklin cast a wider net, including Ovid, Horace, Vergil, Fénelon, Rabelais, Bacon, Dryden, Locke, etc. This competition was met by Bradford, who proceeded to open the largest bookshop in the middle colonies. Franklin and other printers were also publishers — or republishers — who provided such fare as Aristotle, Epictetus, *Pamela, The Sentimental Journey, The Deserted Village, The Wealth of Nations,* Chesterfield's *Letters.*

In addition to excellent lower schools there was "The Academy and College of Philadelphia," which in 1779 became the University of Pennsylvania. Only four other colleges had been started in the colonies earlier: Harvard, William and Mary, Yale, and Princeton. That the growing city of Philadelphia added a fifth was largely due to Franklin, who in 1749 published *Proposals Relating to the Education of Youth in Pennsylvania.* At this college we find a commencement thesis defending the proposition "All men are created equal" fifteen years before the Declaration. While the curriculum was scholastic-classical, the institution also reflected the scientific spirit of the day.

Science. Philadelphia was, in fact, the scientific center of the colonies. Among its prominent men were David Rittenhouse, a farm boy who became an astronomer, John Bartram the botanist, and Morgan, Rush, Shippen and other leaders in medicine. How broadly based and democratic the scientific life was is suggested by the already mentioned Junto led by Franklin. In the group were young men like Godfrey the glazier, Scull the surveyor, Parsons the shoemaker, Maugridge the joiner, men who could apply their skills to making instruments essential to science; also Breitnall, the Quaker merchant, who could establish relations with scientists abroad. Ready to help the group was the aristocrat James Logan, who loved the ancient Classics but also collected in his mansion a superb scientific library.

The most famous "natural philosopher" of the city was of course the ingenious Dr. Franklin himself. Today most people picture Franklin the scientist as a bespectacled colonial flying a kite during a thunderstorm. While the identity of lightning and electricity was his most celebrated discovery, he was in fact fruitful in more than a dozen fields of research, including medicine, astronomy, oceanography, meteorology. Everything roused his curiosity and study, if only the most comfortable way to lie in bed. Again and again he regretted that circumstances kept pushing him into political life and away from the investigation of nature. Truly did Tom Paine say of him: "His mind was ever young; his temper ever serene; science, that never grows gray, was always his mistress." Wedded to public service, he yet served his scientific mistress so well that his contemporaries were inclined to hail him as a second Newton. Along with his quiet passion for study, Franklin entertained a deistic outlook on life, but was too moderate and prudent to display it militantly like Paine. Instead, he went to church. In his heart he agreed with his scientific associate Bartram that "It is through the telescope I see God in his glory."

Many other aspects of colonial Philadelphia could be touched upon, such as its humanitarian activities, or its love of music, both shared by Franklin. But it is already abundantly clear why the city was a happy environment for men of talent and energy — men like Franklin — who could make wise use of its invitation to personal growth, worldly success, and civic responsibility.

MAKING THIRTEEN CLOCKS STRIKE TOGETHER

The golden age of colonial culture, presided over by an aristocracy, soon declined. After flowering in the creative brilliance of Philadelphia, in the charming, studied elegance of the Virginia capital at Williamsburg, and in other centers on the coast from Boston to Charleston, it faded in the disordered climate that set in with the Revolution. In part the American Revolution was a civil war of classes: a democratic uprising, as we shall see, against the wealthy merchants, landed gentry, and others with vested interests. It was also a civil war within the empire, resulting in a new nation that had not been intended. The colonists had long been encouraged in self-government by a mother land distracted by troubles at home, but they heartily wished to stay in the family — to enjoy not American liberties but English liberties in America.

Those who have known a large measure of liberty are not easily content when it is reduced. Trouble arose when the British government tried to exert its right to do less neglecting and more controlling; to reorganize the Empire in such a way as to strengthen it as a whole, make it economically self-sufficient, and regulate it from its center in London. Colonial assemblies quarreled with the royal governors over one problem after another. Acts of Parliament were obeyed grudgingly, or openly flouted. While deeply loyal in sentiment, the colonists had become a strong-willed people resentful of what they considered oppressive interference. They had also become a numerous people. Only 275,000 at the beginning of the century, they had increased to 2,000,000 by 1765, when the population of Great Britain was 8,000,000. They inhabited a great area north and south, and were ready to press into the Mississippi Valley.

Remote from the source of authority, politically mature, large in numbers, and (as Jefferson put it) "with such a country before us to fill with people and with happiness," the Americans moved, as if inevitably, toward nationality. So it seems to us in retrospect. To the colonists, however, it was natural to assume that persuasion and conciliation could suffice to secure the self-development they desired. The pressures from overseas they tried to meet with legal argument. As they interpreted the British constitution, Englishmen who crossed the ocean did not leave their rights as Englishmen behind. Hence, for example, the slogan: "No taxation without representation." But we need not rehearse here the familiar story of the many grievances and persistent protests. Suffice it that by 1773 it was clear enough that on constitutional grounds the colonists could not deal successfully with an imperial government bent upon putting them in their place.

Human Rights. So they shifted the controversy to a broader ground, the broadest possible ground: instead of English law, the law of nature as established by the Creator. John C. Miller has said: "God and Nature, to Americans, were Reason. . . . Until 1776, far from seeking to destroy the Empire, they strove to ensure its prosperity and perpetuation by bringing it into harmony with the laws of nature."

Appeal to the law of nature was strategically strong, since it had general acceptance among the leaders of England. It was associated chiefly with an English thinker with whom we were concerned in connection with deism: John Locke. The colonists found an arsenal of political ideas in his two *Treatises on Civil Government.* In these works Locke had offered an effective justification of the English Revolution of 1688. He might now be used to justify the American Revolution of 1776.

What, asked Locke, must we suppose that human life was like before there was a civil government? In a state of nature, man had perfect freedom and equality. The law of nature and reason restrained him from invading others' rights to life, health, liberty, or possessions. Each man also had the right to punish any who violated this law. Since the right to punish would cause great confusion, men saw the need of coming together and devising a Social Contract, a civil government to interpret the natural law and protect every man in his inalienable natural rights. A group of key quotations will suggest how useful Locke's political reasoning was to the colonists who framed the Declaration of Independence. Said Locke:

> Men being by nature all free, equal, and independent, no one can be put out of this estate and subjected to the political power of another without his own consent.

> The great and chief end . . . of men uniting into commonwealths, and putting themselves under government, is the preservation of their property.

> When by tyranny those in authority forfeit the power the people had put into their hands for quite contrary ends, . . . it devolves to the people, who have a right to resume their original liberty.

The rights most commonly assumed in American discussions were those of life, liberty, and property. The pursuit of happiness was also commonly viewed as a right and was accepted as such, apparently without debate, by the convention which voted the Declaration. If a government violated these natural rights and lost the consent of the governed, the law of nature gave the people the right to alter or abolish that government, to resume their original liberty, and to set up a new government.

The majority of the American people had no desire to translate this theory into radical action. Even nine months after Lexington and Concord the King's health was still being toasted every night in the officers' mess under General Washington. John Adams had to admit that the war was desired by only one third of the population. Who were they? The answer concerns the conflict of classes and of sections which has continued throughout our history.

In general, those who most welcomed war were, as we might expect, those who had least to lose and most to gain. They were the lower class, in the cities and on the farms. While "better off" (according to S. E. Morrison) "than people of their class anywhere else in the world," they had their grievances against the ruling class; for one thing, probably most of them had no vote. Sectionally, those who favored war were inhabitants of the newer country, the West of those days, under-represented in the colonial assemblies. Emotional in politics as in religion, the West contributed largely to the democratic fervor of the period. Coming from this section were their passionate spokesman Patrick Henry and the greatest advocate of democracy, Thomas Jefferson.

Those who wished to avoid war were those who had most to lose and least to gain: the upper class of successful merchants, landed gentry, clergy of the established churches. Sectionally, they were of the East of those days, the seaboard cities and the plain west to the Appalachian foothills. As the propertied and ruling class, they feared that a war against England would bring on a revolution at home. When the war came, they divided, according to conviction or expediency, into a series of groups ranging from professed royalists to active patriots. Of those who remained loyal to the Crown perhaps 50,000 fought on the British side. New York furnished more soldiers to the British than to the Americans. Large numbers of loyalists left the country; others were forced out, their estates confiscated. In all about 100,000 persons, a good portion of the most able and cultivated citizens, were lost from the rising nation just when it needed them most. Among those who chose to stay and serve as patriots during the war and after were men like Otis, Adams, Jay, Dickinson, Pinckney, Rutledge and Washington.

Jefferson. Two men who emerge from the confusion of the period seem about as indispensable as Washington — the radical Jefferson and the conservative Hamilton.

Thomas Jefferson has remained a symbol of the democratic faith to this day, in foreign countries as well as America. The son of a middle-class father and aristocratic mother, himself aristocratic in temper and tastes, he was persistently and increasingly democratic in his political thought. His cultural attainments were early recognized. Said John Adams: "Mr. Jefferson came into Congress in June, 1775, and brought with him a reputation for literature, science, and a happy talent of composition." A year later, when only thirty-three, he was chosen to head the committee that drafted the Declaration of Independence.

To the ringing generalities of the Declaration, Jefferson tried to give concrete meaning and effect by sponsoring measures toward a free, individualistic society in his own State. One was a reform of the laws of inheritance, to distribute land more widely and abolish the aristocracy of birth and wealth. Another disestablished the church in Virginia — "Almighty God has created the mind free" and how can man be truly free unless he has liberty of spirit? Another urged a universal system of education, since Jefferson held that republican government cannot be maintained unless the people's minds are improved. He early advocated the emancipation of Negro slaves, and worked for it till his death. He held freedom of speech and of the press to be indispensable for popular government. State rights he favored not for the sake of the states, but for the sake of individuals, on the ground that the state, as a smaller unit than the nation, is better qualified to assure the liberty of individuals.

This does not exhaust the list of reforms and devices that Jefferson supported in the interest of "a government truly republican." Characteristically, he deplored the "witch-hunt" (the term is his) for radicals and liberals during the Adams administration. And characteristically, at the time of the adoption of the Constitution, he was reconciled only when it was clear that a Bill of Rights would be immediately attached. Typical, too, was his assertion of a right of protest by violence: "a little rebellion, now and then, is a good thing, and as necessary in the political world as storms in the physical."

Plainly, Jefferson's democracy was focused upon the individual. Living in a farming state and a farmer himself, he was strongly drawn by the agrarian philosophy current in his time: the vision of an agricultural society of individuals, virtuous, free, and proud. In a way common among farmers, he distrusted government, especially government from a national center — "Were we directed from Washington when to sow, and when to reap, we should soon want bread." His resentment at government was the greater when it came from the imperial authority in London. He had a nature peculiarily suited to his momentous task in the Declaration of Independence, and to his role as a perennial foe of tyranny. Yet his reliance upon the free individual involved the risk of having no government at all but only anarchy, so that a modern historical scholar was constrained to say that "Had we attempted to follow Jefferson completely, the nation might not only not have continued but not have survived its first decade."

Hamilton. Had we, on the other hand, attempted to follow Hamilton completely, the nation might have had a government like that of eighteenth-century England, monarchical and aristocratic, or like the "Leviathan" state of Hobbes, highly centralized and authoritative, which in our time we call the totalitarian state. Yet this must not blind us to his immense contribution. Hamilton had much to do with the fact that there was a nation at all, and that it did survive. During the war, the government of the sovereign colonies through their Congress was so feeble that in 1780 Hamilton could say of the army: "It is now a mob rather than an army; without clothing, without provision, without morals, without discipline." In the same year, even before the weak

Articles of Confederation had been adopted, he proposed the Constitutional Convention which eventually met half a dozen years later. Hamilton was quite right in observing to Washington that "The centrifugal is much stronger than the centripetal force in these States; the seeds of disunion much more numerous than those of union." In the happy phrase of John Adams, the problem was to make thirteen clocks strike together. This was also the view of Franklin, who had warned long before that if the colonies did not hang together they would hang separately.

While we can easily see now, as Hamilton did then, the need of a strong central government to assure union and stability in peace and war, we are not likely to share Hamilton's intense fear of democracy. Yet he was only saying what nearly all eighteenth-century gentlemen were thinking when he argued before the convention:

> All communities divide themselves into the few and the many. The first are the rich and well born, the other the mass of the people. The voice of the people has been said to be the voice of God; and, however generally this maxim has been quoted and believed, it is not true to fact. The people are turbulent and changing; they seldom judge or determine right.

As a realist (cynic?) answering the idealist (dreamer?) Hamilton went so far, on another occasion, as to exclaim, "The people! — the people is a great beast!"

The Constitution did not give Hamilton what he had proposed: a president and senate chosen for life, together with state governors appointed by the president for life. But he supported it as an acceptable compromise. At least "the imprudence of democracy" was to be curbed in some measure by a system of checks and balances. According to Woodrow Wilson, among others, this elaborate arrangement of political forces opposed to each other but producing an equilibrium while they are kept moving is to be accounted for ultimately by the Newtonian physics. The physical universe being an intricate mechanism like a watch, it seemed possible for human reason to devise a carefully balanced political watch. The instrument did provide a way to balk a hasty and impulsive popular will, and reconciled state and nation by means of federation. In 1760 an English traveler had opined that "fire and water are not more heterogeneous than the different colonies." Yet before the 1800's federation was a durable fact, and by the middle 1900's success in the New World seriously suggested federal union in the Old — a United States of Europe.

Was Hamilton actually so zealous for union and stability or was he primarily intent upon government in the interest of the capitalist class? The question is still debated by historians. At least we may say with assurance that, as Jefferson had seen that an agricultural society would make for free individuals, Hamilton saw that an industrial society would make for firm government. By various contrivances and with extraordinary ability he formed a capitalist class and founded the middle-class capitalist state that we know. America was to be less and less a nation of Jefferson's small farmers, more and more a nation of "Big Business" developed by industrialists and financiers.

The West. This process did not retard, however, the development of the West. The interest which men like Franklin and Jefferson had in agriculture and the West was justified afresh by settlement of the fertile prairies of the Mississippi basin. After the Revolution the new nation began in earnest the occupation of the continent. Not long after the war of 1812 Indiana and Illinois, Mississippi and Alabama, were admitted to the Union. The good life seemed to beckon westward, as a single quotation will illustrate. Writing to a brother in England in 1818, one Samuel Crabtree says enticingly:

> This is the country for a man to enjoy himself: Ohio, Indiana, and the Missouri Territory; where you may see prairie 60 miles long and 10 broad, not a stick nor a stone in them, at two dollars an acre, that will produce 70 to 100 bushels of Indian corn per acre; too rich for wheat or any other kind of grain. . . . The poorest family has a cow or two and some sheep and in the fall can gather as many apples and peaches as serve the year round. Good rye whiskey; apple and peach brandy. . . . The poorest families adorn the table three times a day like a wedding dinner.

Lacking in this picture are other aspects of the agricultural West: grinding toil, lawlessness, debt, problems of supply and marketing, together with an irritated disrelish for Eastern bankers, lawyers, and politicians. Yet on the whole the people of the new West had a good way of life, characterized by liberty, equality, and fraternity, as might be expected where nature was bounteous, property was widely distributed, and all men could vote. Western and Southern small farmers, along with mechanics in the Eastern cities, at length sent to the White House a farmer, a man of the people, "Old Hickory." Small wonder that Jackson's worshipping followers, at his inauguration, acted like ruffians, so that Justice Story deemed that "The reign of King Mob seemed triumphant," while a much perturbed society lady was reminded of "descriptions I have read of the mobs in the Tuileries and at Versailles." The leadership of the Virginia and Massachusetts aristocracy was over.

A CULTURAL ANCHOR: THE CLASSICAL TRADITION

People who divorce themselves from one tradition have usually become attached to another. The aristocratic and the educated classes of the eighteenth century, gradually alienated from the tradition of Christian devotion, found more and more satisfaction in the worldly tradition of Classical humanism. The Puritan Age had prized but subordinated the Classics; the Neo-Classic Age found in them the main cultural anchor of its rationalism, its unbounded belief that human reason is competent to deal with the world and life. Had not the Greeks and the Romans lived a life so rational, so clear-eyed, so moderate and sane, that they set a standard for all time? Even if pure reason was the ultimate authority, were not reason and the ancients essentially the same? Pure reason had triumphed in Newton, scientist of the physical universe, and in Locke, scientist of man, but far behind these modern thinkers lay a whole world of wisdom and beauty, a constant source of guidance and delight. The history, philosophy, and literature of the ancients did not seem remote or antiquated, but intimately present because permanently enlightening.

Before entering college at the age of fourteen or fifteen, American students in this period were expected to be able to speak in Latin, and in college they were fined for not speaking in Latin, except during recreation. Latin was the language of most of their textbooks and lectures. The New Testament in Greek was required for admission, and in Greek they also studied Homer and Longinus. In Latin the chief authors were Cicero, Vergil, and Horace. A continued interest in the classics after college was usual. "Every accomplished gentleman," says Wertenbaker, "was supposed to know his Homer and his Ovid, and in conversation was put to shame if he failed to recognize a quotation from either." Self-made men like Franklin, without benefit of college, derived more from the ancient world than one would expect, but the more typical Founding Fathers meditated long and deeply on the ancient patterns of democracy and republics, and Jefferson was only expressing a frequent view of his time when he said of ancient literature: "The Greeks and Romans have left us the present models which exist of fine composition, whether we examine them as works of reason, or style, or fancy. . . . To read the Latin and Greek authors in the original is a sublime luxury." In their literary taste the men of the Age of Reason felt themselves to be descendants not of Chaucer, Spenser, and Shakespeare, but of Homer, Sophocles, Vergil, and Horace.

To pass from ancient to contemporary literature did not then mean, as it would today, a vast cultural leap, for contemporary writers purported, in the main, to imitate the ancients. The tradition coming down from the Greeks and Romans had been rationalized and formalized into a new classicism, first in seventeenth-century France, then in eighteenth-century England. Because the culture of America was English, American readers relied heavily upon such masters of the Neo-Classic Age as Addison, Steele, Pope, Swift and Dr. Johnson. The authoritarian confidence of neo-classicism, lingering among Federalists into the nineteenth century, was well expressed by a literary minister of Boston, Theodore Dehon, who said: "It is with literature as with government. Neither is a subject of perpetual experiment. The principles of both are fixed."

Poetry. Modern poetry, to Americans of the period, meant chiefly the sort of verse written in England by Alexander Pope and his followers. Pope reigned supreme on our side of the Atlantic through the eighteenth century and beyond. Early in the century Mather Byles compared him with Homer. Even James Russell Lowell, who was born in 1819 and belongs in the next period, could say, "I was brought up in the old superstition that he was the greatest poet that ever lived." Critics extolled Pope for his ethical sentiments, his keen satire, and the "musick" of his verse. William Bentley, in Salem, inserted in his commonplace book these lines describing the work of the master:

Though gay as mirth, as curious thought sedate,
As elegance polite, as power elate;
Profound as reason, and as justice clear;
Soft as compassion, yet as truth severe;
As bounty copious, as persuasion sweet,
Like nature various, and like art complete.

To eighteenth-century Americans it seemed that Pope's poetry harmonized with life as they were trying to live it: a poetry of rationality, clarity, moderation, elegance, decorum. It was, in truth, a poetry well suited to the age of the minuet, of salons, of formal gardens, of Georgian and Classical architecture. The fashionable verse form was the heroic couplet as perfected by Pope, regular, brilliant, neatly phrased, faultlessly groomed — should not poetic truth, like ladies and gentlemen, be dressed to advantage? The substance beneath should be unchanging Nature — that is, human nature as it always is. The art of poetry, like the art of politics, should express universal, self-evident truths:

. . . Nature to advantage drest,
What oft was thought, but ne'er so well exprest,
Something whose truth convinc'd at sight we find.

When they themselves composed verse, Americans followed, awkwardly, the English styles of the day. New England's poets in the 1730's, says H. B. Parkes, "described Harvard commencements in the style of 'The Rape of the Lock,' or else they sang of the charms of Women and the delights of Marriage in the borrowed strains of Matthew Prior. John Adams [the Rev. John Adams] gave Pope a Puritan coloring, putting psalms into heroic couplets and describing Cotton Mather's entry into heaven, surrounded by attendant angels, chubby and florid as on a Versailles ceiling." Some better things in the neo-classic vein were achieved late in the period by the Connecticut Wits, but most of their work was superficially patriotic, ineptly ambitious, and dull. On the whole, American neo-classic verse showed so little original power that there is hardly occasion to attempt here an account of its development, though we shall have something to say presently of Freneau as a transitional figure between neo-classicism and romanticism.

Prose. The prose was excellent. In that "age of prose and reason" (as Matthew Arnold called the eighteenth century)

Americans learned to write an admirable prose of reason — a prose of statement and argument, not of description and narration — a prose serving practical rather than aesthetic ends. It reflected the discipline of twenty years of discussion before the Revolution, when the streets, taverns, and homes of America were filled with talk of politics, local and imperial. By 1775 it was possible for the elder William Pitt, speaking in the House of Lords, to say of the political papers coming from America: "For solidity of reasoning, force of sagacity, and wisdom of conclusion, no nation or body of men can stand in preference to the General Congress in Philadelphia." During the Revolutionary period alone, political pamphlets came pouring from the presses till they reached an estimated 2,000. Sometimes these little books had public readings, in a militia camp or at meetings of the Sons of Liberty; sometimes they had public burnings, if written by loyalists. A good example of the radical pamphlets is Paine's *Common Sense,* which argued that the colonists, having gone so far, must embrace freedom. This brilliantly conceived piece of propaganda was greeted with enthusiasm by leaders and public alike, sold over 100,000 copies within three months, and had much to do with the eventual break with England. But the masterpiece of all this political writing was Jefferson's Declaration of Independence. The colonies had a writer equal to the greatest occasion of the century. After independence had been achieved and the dark critical years had offered the challenge met by the Constitution, came another distinguished work of civic literature: *The Federalist,* written in support of the Constitution by Hamilton with the aid of Madison and Jay.

The leading prose writer of the period, however, was Benjamin Franklin. An able political writer, he often showed a waggish or satirical turn of mind. Like his political, his non-political writings were intended in one way or another to serve a useful purpose. They included his Almanac, his scientific works, and the earliest masterpiece of American literature — his *Autobiography.* This guarded yet intimate revelation of a personality comes to us refreshingly from a period when attention was fixed on ideas and principles and on men in general rather than on the individual and his experiences. Franklin also wrote periodical essays, with a didactic purpose, in the manner of the English *Spectator,* and tried his hand at "bagatelles," informal essays with a French wit and urbanity. And he was America's best letter-writer (with Jefferson next after him) in a century that excelled in the letter as a supplement to the art of conversation.

Writers in America as in England were now employing a new prose style. In England style had been reshaped, for an age of science and politics, in the interest of greater clarity and simplicity. Earlier English prose had abounded in involved sentence structure, complicated parentheses, Latinized diction, fantastic phrasing, pedantry, luxuriance — at its worst "a glaring chaos and wild heap." A new pattern was forming when in 1667, as Thomas Sprat tells us, the Royal Society expected its members to use "a close, naked, natural way of speaking; positive expressions, clear senses, a native easiness, bringing all things as near the mathematical plainness as they can." The new prose was perfected by Dryden, with a fine balance of ease and energy, and later polished by Addison. America imported not only the ideas of the eighteenth century but the neo-classic style of Addison, Swift, Goldsmith, and the rest. One can readily see the movement toward order, lucidity, precision, ease, and simplicity by contrasting the writings of Cotton Mather and Franklin.

Sentimentalism. In style as in substance, the imaginative prose of the period was far inferior to the practical prose. Whereas in politics America had much to say and said it well, in the field of the novel American readers were generally content with the offerings of English masters such as Defoe, Richardson, Fielding, Sterne, Smollett. Or they frowned upon all novel reading as endangering one's morals. Naturally, the writing of fiction did not thrive. Apparently the first American novel was *The Power of Sympathy* (1789) by William Hill Brown, and the most popular was Mrs. Rowson's *Charlotte Temple.* These illustrate the taste for sentimentalism, for tenderness and tears, which flouted the reigning rationalism, though less than in England. Typically, our early novelists celebrated the natural goodness and benevolence of the human heart, and pictured characters interested in sensibility, seduction, and suicide. Sentimental in another way were the novels of Charles Brockden Brown — the best known is *Wieland.* Reflecting the so-called "Gothic" school in England, they focused upon mystery, horrors, and thrills. Like the novel, the drama and theater were widely disapproved. The first original play put on by a professional company was *The Prince of Parthia,* a "tragedy of blood" in blank verse by Thomas Godfrey, acted in Philadelphia in 1767, and the first American comedy, *The Contrast* by Royall Tyler, was produced in New York twenty years later. Other plays followed — William Dunlap wrote fifty-three. But as A. H. Quinn has said, "when we consider the difficulties under which the playwright labored in America the wonder is that any work was done."

In making feeling the measure, instead of reason, sentimentalism and melodrama were preparing the way for romanticism. The transition is perhaps clearest in the poetry. Even the neo-classic Connecticut Wits, in their nationalistic enthusiasm, were unawares leading toward the romantic insistence upon a native rather than classical tradition. The best example, however, is the leading poet of the period. Philip Freneau, poised, so to speak, between two centuries. As a deist he subscribed, like Tom Paine, to the religion of reason. As a democrat he was, again like Paine, an ardent radical. Feeling called upon to make poetry as well as prose serve politics, he devoted a large proportion of his verse to the cause of, first, American independence, next the French Revolution, and then the party of Jefferson, commonly using the method of satire. But his real interest and talent lay elsewhere. He preferred to write poetry rather than versified propaganda, and managed to write enough of it to show what he could do. While retaining much that was typical of the neo-classic regime, such as direct moralizing, conventional diction ("vernal showers"), and facile personification ("Liberty, Celestial Maid"), he could also write simply and naturally, sometimes with delicate precision. In his lyrical poems he is akin to such English "pre-romantics" as Gray, Collins, and Cowper. As they pointed toward Wordsworth and Coleridge, so he toward Bryant and Poe. Thus, in "The Wild Honeysuckle" there is a sensitive response to nature, in "The Beauties of Vera Cruz" freshness of sensuous appeal and the charm of the strange and remote, in "The House of Night" the ability to invest the horrible and the supernatural with imaginative energy. By writing of this sort Freneau takes us to the threshold of a new literary age, an age of romanticism.

THE ROMANTIC MOVEMENT

Individualism in Feeling and Imagination

"The world exists for you. . . . Build therefore your own world"
— EMERSON

Youth, said Emerson, is romantic. It was perhaps fortunate that when our writers were starting a national literature, Europe was communicating romantic enthusiasms and America itself was full of youthful vigor. We easily forget that America was old before it was young. The first settlers brought with them from the old world a mature culture. Later colonials naturally maintained close relations with the mother country, reflecting its altering patterns of living and thinking. Successively they were Elizabethan explorers like Captain John Smith, builders of Puritan plantations like John Winthrop, English-style country gentlemen like William Byrd, statesmen with scientific interests like Franklin and Jefferson. Engrossed in tremendous practical tasks, they wrote a practical prose, relying on importation for such *belles-lettres* as they desired. When political independence came, they could not create overnight an independent literary culture. The efforts of the Connecticut Wits and Freneau were premature.

A YOUNG DEMOCRACY

After the War of 1812, however, the new nation set about building a civilization and culture of its own, with the self-consciousness and exuberance of youth. "It was America's awkward age," says Samuel E. Morison. The "child who had left his parents' roof, the marvellous boy who had proclaimed great truths (or perhaps delusion) to a candid world, was now a gawky hobbledehoy." In a similar vein James T. Adams remarks upon "the youthfulness of the whole period," "its adolescence — the sudden discovery of romance, of culture, of altruism, of optimism, of self-reliance, and the sense of one's own individuality." These are broad generalizations. Let us collect a few particulars to sustain them, let us examine a few features of the ebullient civilization which was the environment of our writers from Irving to Whitman.

Their America was expanding at a spectacular rate. In 1820 the people of the United States numbered 9,638,000; in 1860 they had increased to 31,443,000, owing partly to immigration. Even more amazing was the expansion in territory. By 1821, as many as eleven states had been added to the original thirteen. From New England and the Upper South pioneers moved into the rich valley of the Ohio and Mississippi. Chicago, in 1833, had a population of only 350, but by 1870 about 300,000. When California was annexed from Mexico in 1848, wide open spaces beckoned all the way to the Pacific.

East and Middle West were linked by the Erie Canal, and then came the age of railroads — the Baltimore and Ohio, the Pennsylvania, and others, till by 1860 the iron rails covered 30,000 miles. The general aspect of the country was still agricultural; yet by 1860 the value of its manufactures equalled that of its crops. Sectional differences were so great that, as one historian has said, the civilizations of North and South were as wide apart as those of Canada and Mexico today. The South was now the Cotton Kingdom, with white fields, black slaves, and an attachment to Sir Walter Scott, in whose novels, as Morison puts it, "the cotton lord and his lady found a romantic mirror of their life and ideals." But it was the democratic West — the land of the advancing frontier — that seemed the America of the future. "Europe," said Emerson, "stretches to the Alleghanies; America lies beyond." We may well think of the winning of the West as a sort of romanticism of action, reaching its climax in the discovery of gold in California, from which the fever of sudden riches spread rapidly to the East and even to Europe. The speed with which the West was effectively settled is a main feature of this period. In vain did John Quincy Adams, like Jefferson before him, wish to avoid the evils of a too rapid expansion by preserving the Western lands for a planned development over centuries.

And yet in a very real sense it may be said that the industrial East, not the agricultural West, was the America of the future. Especially after the Civil War, ours was to be a business civilization. Even within the period we are now considering, the pattern was well established. The Industrial Revolution arrived in a land as rich in resources as it was vast in extent, a land with a laissez-faire economy that made the competition for success and wealth unbridled. A succession of newly invented machines was the means to a tremendous increase in productivity and trade. By 1840 the United States had 1200 cotton textile factories, chiefly in New England, and the pig-iron industry, centered in eastern Pennsylvania, raised its production tenfold in the forty years preceding 1850. The crops of the Middle West were pouring east in ever growing volume. Assuredly America was the land of opportunity.

Was it also, in Washington Irving's phrase, the "Land of the Almighty Dollar"? If so, it was hardly because Americans were peculiarly sinful in their love of riches, for better examples of unrestrained materialism and its attendant abuses could be found in industrial England. But there is no question that riches seemed astonishingly easy. "In the seething America of the 1830's and 1840's," says a prominent historian, "both immigrant and old American felt that, with just a little luck, fortune might be waiting for him just around the corner. Hadn't Astor made $20,-000,000, Girard left $6,000,000, while men in every community were evidently getting rich on a large if less spectacular scale?"

Without restraint by class or government, Americans pursued business with abandon. A traveler described New York about 1840 as "the busiest community that any man could desire to live in. In the streets all is hurry and bustle; the very carts, instead of being drawn by horses at a walking pace, are often met at a gallop, and always in a brisk trot. The whole of the population seen in the streets seems to enjoy this bustle, and add to it by their own rapid pace." Travelers generally frowned upon this American speed, as in the eighteenth century they had deplored American indolence. Visitors from England, in the East, looked in vain for public parks, games and sports, or walking in the country. As work had been a virtue among the Puritans, so now the making of money was conceived as a patriotic duty, a contribution to the rapid development of the country. A leisure class seemed inappropriate when the man of inherited wealth, as an observer tells us, saw "nobody about him not engaged in business." Cultural activities were commonly disparaged because they reduced the speed of money-making; literature and music were more suitable for women. Everything seemed to conspire to encourage a type of businessman full of drive and zest in his vocation but otherwise empty. A crass plutocracy was taking the place of the old aristocracy.

While the prosperous were growing in wealth and power, and the common man was comfortable and could hope to be prosperous, Americans became brash and boastful. They scorned the Old-World monarchies overseas and feared no nation under the sun. Seeing the rapid progress of the country in material power, in science and technology, apparently in every department of life, they readily transformed the eighteenth century idea of progress into a religion, and envisaged for their land a resplendent future. The only dark cloud in sight was slavery, but 99 per cent of Northern businessmen, it has been estimated, believed that if the North held its tongue and kept its fingers out, the problem would somehow solve itself without ruining business and breaking up the Union.

National Self-Reliance. The spirit of nationalism throve along with this zest for business expansion and optimism over the future. In America as in Europe, the cosmopolitanism of the eighteenth century was followed by the nationalism of the nineteenth. It emerged symbolically during the War of 1812 in the guise of "Uncle Sam," and was expressed in the patriotic gaiety and bombastic oratory of Fourth of July celebrations. In a mood we would now call isolationist, America turned its back on the Atlantic and in the 1820's announced the Monroe Doctrine that the Americas were for Americans. By the middle of the century the slogan "Manifest Destiny" suggested rather that the Americas were for the Americans of the United States. In their patriotic zeal and their appetite for expansion, many people came to feel that the great American democracy should include territories that nature seemed to have intended for her: Canada, the Caribbean, Mexico, Central America, the islands of the Pacific.

Thus an expansive self-reliance showed itself on the national as on the individual level. It showed itself also, between these two extremes, on the level of section and state. A section of the United States, as the historian Turner put it, is a "potential nation," or "the faint image of a European nation." It is a part of our national domain conscious of its own tradition, material interests, social ideals, as different from those of other sections. Before the Civil War the country had four sections: East (the old North), South, Middle West, and Far West. The secession of the South was a violent assertion of self-reliance. There was a similar sense of unity and pride within the individual state. It was not so much the South that seceded as one southern state after another. The great war that followed substantially settled the relation of states' rights, sectional interests, and the Union.

In young America, as we have noted, the prizes were open to all. The eighteenth century had stressed the "free" in the concept of "free and equal," especially the free, rational mind, and the Revolution brought political freedom. The early national period was zealous not only for the free but for the equal. Equality was dramatized by the Jacksonian upheaval. From this time dates the custom of telling the American boy that someday he may be President of the United States. In many ways the middle-class leadership that took the place of the aristocracy flattered and served the common man, the laborer and farmer. It is significant that the Whig party in 1840 deemed it wise to ignore the patrician origin of William Henry Harrison and to picture him, in the campaign, as seated before a log cabin with a barrel of hard cider. State after state extended the ballot, and an effective public school system was undertaken in earnest. There were many workers for humanitarian reforms: prison reform, temperance, the granting of women's rights, the abolition of slavery, the last of which increasingly cast the others in shadow. To the old conservative families of the East and South, it seemed that they were living out of context in this century of the common man, not to say of commonness. But there were also patricians like Ralph Waldo Emerson who accepted the changing world and welcomed "the near, the low, the common."

Native Roots of Romanticism. Despite young America's growing absorption in business and material progress, an adequate public for the new literary movement was prepared in a number of ways. The romantic impulse from Europe might well have proved fruitless if there had not been strong American roots favoring romanticism. Some of them have already been indicated. One was America's patriotic nationalism, crude but capable of idealistic refinement. Another was its democratic society, with far more liberty, equality, and fraternity than in the aristocratic eighteenth century. Another was the emphasis on the single man, the self-reliant man, encouraged both by a laissez-faire economy and the individualism of the frontier. Another was the mood of optimism natural in a land of opportunity. We shall come to see more clearly how romanticism gave these new meaning.

But the most vital preparation for such writers as Emerson, Thoreau, Hawthorne, Melville, and Whitman was a religious spirit that goes back to the men and women who settled America. Puritans, Quakers, Anglicans and others had left in the American mind an enduring reverence and a sensitive conscience. The worldliness and rationalism of the age of Franklin could bank the old religious fires, but not quench them. In the early nineteenth century revivals flamed up afresh; more important perhaps was a piety expressed in day-by-day observances. As we read in an autobiography by S. G. Goodrich, "In most families the first exercise of the morning was reading the Bible, followed by prayer, at which all were assembled, including the servants and helpers of the kitchen and the farm." Calvinists were still far from extinct, especially in the country, while the Unitarians were well established among the upper classes in cities and town. If Unitarianism was related on one side to Locke and eighteenth-century rationalism, it was related on the other to Emerson and the Transcendentalist movement. Already in the words of William

Ellery Channing, the great leader of the Unitarians, one can see the thoughts of Emerson and his contemporaries emerging. "We must start in religion," Channing had said, "from our own souls. In these is the fountain of all divine truth. . . . The soul is the spring of our knowledge of God."

Often closely connected with these various types of religious devotion was a hunger of the mind, shown by the Lyceum and other schemes for popular lectures, which spread over the country. In 1834, when this cultural movement was at its height, the local lyceums totaled about 3000. A favorite speaker was Ralph Waldo Emerson, whose tours took him even beyond the Mississippi in midwinter. Meanwhile, in publications, literary taste had long been nourished, after a fashion, by sentimental and Gothic novels and dramas. Poor though they were in quality they opened the way for something better by stirring sympathetic feelings and an appetite for the strange and mysterious.

To preserve what was strong in the spiritual and imaginative background, to deepen what was shallow, to refine and diversify what was crude and over-simple, to transform what was faintly felt into a whole new vision of life and art — this was to be the task of the literary artists of the romantic movement.

THE ROMANTIC REVOLT

The more sensitive minds, in America as in Europe, felt that the Age of Reason had run its course. They were less and less comfortable in the world of ideas established so long ago by Newton, Locke, and Pope. They were profoundly dissatisfied with a rationalism and neo-classicism daily more remote from their experience. Yet, unless somehow dislodged, the old scheme of ideas would linger forever. A new movement must overcome the old. In the political realm there was no real problem, since the democratic ideas of the eighteenth century were still held valid, needing only fuller expression in theory and practice. But in the vast realm of thought and feeling concerning the deity, and nature, and human nature and destiny, and an art suited to a new outlook on life — here a tremendous change seemed called for.

A New Set of Affirmations. Man is something more than a thinking machine in a machine universe. We cannot be content with ideas clear and consistent at the expense of truth; something is always left out. Reality is too large and diverse, too vital and fluid, to be compassed by cool reason. Nor is common sense sufficient; it may be the way to wealth and easy living, but not to high thinking or deep feeling. The world we live in is not a dead machine, but rather a living, breathing being. God is not outside the universe, forgetting and forgotten, but in it and in us, an immanent presence. Man does not come into the world as a blank page to be written on, but as a spirit trailing clouds of glory. What then is a poet? Not a polite tailor in words, dressing nature and human nature to advantage, not a wit writing an artificial language for town and court, but a man speaking to all men of our common humanity and the experiences of the heart. He is an inspired bard, a creative, original genius expressing his innermost self, which is always taking new forms, reshaping its world in new visions of truth and beauty. As Josiah Royce was later to sum up the German romantic school, it proclaimed:

> Trust your genius; follow your noble heart; change your doctrine whenever your heart changes, and change your heart often. Such is the practical creed of the romanticists. The world, you see, is after all the world of the inner life. . . . The world is essentially what men of genius make it. Let us be men of genius, and make what we choose.

The secret of life, in the new outlook, lies not in the head but in the heart. We are to seek reality not through conscious thought but through immediate intuitive perception. The kingdom of God is within. The head brought only doubt and barrenness, but we may trust the heart — feeling — desire — the yearning for fulfillment — the Faustian spirit of aspiration. The human spirit must be emancipated, freed from the tyranny of everything exterior to itself, whether this was a Calvinistic dogma of depravity, or a cramping rationalism, or a common sense obsession with the pots and pans of practical life. Freed from these it might regain the sense of wonder, the bloom of the world; might dwell upon the strange, the mysterious, the miraculous, might hope for a revelation here and now.

The inner life and its needs, in the romantic view, are not identical in all men. If men are born free and equal in worth as human beings, they are also born different, no two of them alike. Each should therefore be true to himself, express his uniquely valuable self. It is hardly mere accident that the new words compounded with *self* in the nineteenth century were not often like the old *self-conceit, self-esteem, self-denial,* which now seemed unpleasant, but rather *self-expression, self-realization, self-culture, self-help, self-reliance,* which seemed more attractive.

An International Movement. The Romantic Movement was strikingly international. In America, as in all the major countries of Europe, it had native roots but was fertilized and brought to fruition by foreign influences. Each country sought a national culture, an organic expression of its special "genius." As a result, we can observe differing interests and emphases in the romanticisms of England, Germany, France, Spain, Russia, the United States. But the resemblances are at least equally obvious. National self-reliance did not mean isolationism of the mind. The thinkers, artists, critics who led the way used suggestions wherever they found them, not only in native experience but in any land where a renewal was in progress. In France they looked largely to England, in England to Germany, in Germany to England, for ideas and attitudes, for visions of the good life, for the inspiration of imaginative art. In the United States they looked to many European countries, above all England and Germany, where the movement flourished about two decades earlier than in the New World.

In Germany they saw philosophy given a new start by Kant, one of the great thinkers of all time, whose critiques, as they understood, had demolished the Age of Reason at its very foundations and made possible the erection of a new structure in harmony with man's high aspirations. Starting from Kant, Fichte had declared his "world-positing ego" — an inner spiritual activity which enables each one of us to build his own world. Then came the poetic philosopher Schelling, with his idea, dear to many romanticists, that spirit within man is the same as spirit within nature. Along with the philosophers were fascinating writers of literature. There was not only the towering figure of Goethe — one of Emerson's "Representative Men" — but a whole Romantic School, bold and brilliant (Tieck, Novalis, the Schlegel brothers, etc.). Here then was a dazzling array of systematic thinkers and creative writers who had broken with the eighteenth century and at length carried the movement, as Carlyle said, to completion. It is true that Americans often knew them only slightly and understood them ill — much as Marx and Freud have fared in our time. Yet at least they were convinced, by Coleridge and Carlyle, that Germany had led in a direction they wanted to go in their own way.

In England too they saw the old thought and literary art dissolved, the new taking form. If many were convinced that the core of the movement was in Germany, all American writers were naturally drawn to England by habit, sentiment, and language: what they found could be readily assimilated. Wordsworth illustrated for them a poetic sensibility expressed in simple language, profound in feeling and imagination, in contact with the spiritual "Presences" of Nature (instead of the deistic "absentee" Creator) and with the lives of common folk glorified by human dignity. Coleridge, for the Transcendentalists at any rate, made his impression chiefly through his prose writings, in which the new German philosophy and the tradition of Platonism were combined with religious earnestness. He seemed to validate the intuitive and imaginative powers of man that rationalism had so long neglected. And then there was the young romantic Carlyle, escaping from both Scottish Calvinism and the Age of Reason with the aid of his beloved Germans. He gave an example of hatred of artificiality and sham, of love of sincerity and wonder, of awareness of the Infinite, the vast reservoir of power upon which great men draw so much and lesser men too little.

Although Carlyle's *Sartor Resartus* was first published in book form in America, with a preface by his friend Emerson, oddly enough Emerson failed to mention him when, in 1840, he sketched the course of the new movement. "This love of the Infinite," he wrote in *The Dial*, ". . . this new love of the vast, always native in Germany, was imported into France by De Staël, appeared in England in Coleridge, Wordsworth, Byron, Shelley, . . . and finds a most genial climate in the American mind." Many other traits of European romanticism were acclimatized by American writers looking for incitement, doctrine, example. Not content merely to look from afar, many of them made the Atlantic crossing, in days when it was slow and uncomfortable, to see the Old World intimately with their own eyes. Of our thirteen chief writers, Irving to Whitman, only three did not know Europe at first hand. Clearly, the War of Independence did not end, among our intellectuals, the sense of an Atlantic Community.

CONCORD AND OTHER CENTERS

"Who reads an American book?" Sydney Smith's question in the *Edinburgh Review* of 1820 was painfully galling to Americans. They were, as Irving said, "a young people, necessarily an imitative one," but they were also sensitive and ambitious. They knew only too well how little they had written to merit British approbation in the two hundred years since the Plymouth plantation, or in the thirty-seven years since the recognition of the American Republic. Yet in fact a national literature was beginning in the city of New York at this very time, as witness: *The Sketch Book* by Irving in 1819 and 1820, *The Spy* by Cooper in 1821. Bryant was soon to join them.

These three early romantics, born in the eighteenth century, did most of their best work during the years 1810-1835, which William Charvat has called "the period of the incubation of romanticism." The genial pen of Irving, schooled in neoclassic prose, made the picturesque past of Europe and America live. Cooper, while no stylist, could tell a story and describe graphically the forest frontier with its rather too "noble" Indians. Bryant, assimilating the English pre-romantics and Wordsworth, wrote, with poetic dignity and breadth, of nature and death. With these three "Knickerbocker" writers were associated others prominent in their day but now generally forgotten.

Most of the "Knickerbocker" writers were drawn to New York by advantages it offered the man of letters. Intent though the metropolis was on commercial enterprise, its wealth made for cultural advance, for publishing houses, magazines, newspapers (including the *Evening Post* long edited by Bryant). In 1820 the city's population was 123,000; by 1840 it was 312,000. Early in the century it had the air of a country town, with half-built streets — a "hobbledehoy metropolis" Cooper called it. As seen by Charles Dickens in 1842, it was still a straggling city, low and flat, without plumbing, its waterfront bristling with masts, its streets roamed by scavenger hogs; but it also had many stately residences furnished and adorned with silverware and oil portraits. Old families, Dutch and English, saw the cherished past fading as the *nouveau riche* took charge. The Hudson Valley market-town was becoming the urban symbol of a fast-moving young America devoted to commerce, industry, and finance.

Concord. It is a far cry from the solid materialism of New York to the airy idealism of Concord. The place was only a village, one of thousands in the nation, yet in it was a stir of mind and spirit that affected American life and letters for decades.

Less than twenty miles from Boston, Concord was a community of 2,000 when Thoreau was born there — he was the only native in the literary group. The village was on a quietly gliding stream, bordered by dwarf willows and wild grape vines (whence the cultivated Concord grape). Meadows led to uplands and small lakes called ponds. Walden Pond, where Emerson owned woodland, was less than a two-mile walk from his house on the Lexington road at the edge of town. In another part of the rambling white village was the Old Manse, where Emerson and then Hawthorne lived for a time, close to the hallowed spot at the river where

. . . once the embattled farmers stood
And fired the shot heard round the world.

In this historic association Concord may symbolize for us the nationalistic impulse of our romanticism. But its roots go much deeper, to the time when Old Concord was the first inland plantation of the Massachusetts Colony and had as its first minister an ancestor of Emerson. To this pleasant little town, where plain living and high thinking had always seemed natural, Emerson came to reside in 1834, followed after some years by Bronson Alcott, Ellery Channing (poet nephew of the Unitarian leader), and Hawthorne. At times Margaret Fuller lived there, and at all times Concord-born Thoreau.

Before the Concord group began to form, Massachusetts had nothing comparable to the activity of the Connecticut Wits or the New York group of early romantics. In the whole state, Emerson remarked dryly in his journal, "from 1790 to 1820, there was not a book, a speech, a conversation, or a thought," and for the years after 1820 he could name only Channing, Webster, and Edward Everett. But the Transcendental movement, for which Concord was to be famous, was gathering, and by 1836 burst forth with vigor. In September 1836, Emerson, Alcott, George Ripley, F. H. Hedge and two others "chanced to confer together," as Hedge recalled, "on the state of current opinion in theology and philosophy, which we agreed in thinking very unsatisfactory. . . . What we strongly felt was dissatisfaction with the reigning sensuous philosophy, dating from Locke, on which our Unitarian theology was based." Hedge went on to say that, thanks to the writings of Coleridge and Carlyle, "there was a promise in the air of a new era of intellectual life." Later meetings were attended at one time or another by Orestes Brownson, Margaret Fuller, Jones Very, Thoreau, and others of less interest today. These informal gatherings led to a quarterly magazine, *The Dial*, edited by Margaret Fuller and later Emerson, which ran for four years. They also helped to create an atmosphere that produced, in time, such social experiments as the "ideal" communities of Brook Farm and Fruitlands, as well as Thoreau's one-man experiment at Walden Pond.

Transcendentalism. What was this "Transcendentalism" that everyone was talking about in eastern Massachusetts and few professed to understand? It has often been described in a single phrase as "Romanticism on Puritan soil." What this implies will be clearer when we come to survey the romantic view of life and art. Suffice it to say here that the Transcendental movement was a spiritual affirmation and an intellectual effort to restore — but in a vastly changed form — the high conception of the human soul and destiny in which Puritan New England had been schooled so long but which a rationalism based on the senses had overlaid with a burden become intolerable. It is a return to something like the flashes of divinity in the poems of Edward Taylor, or Jonathan Edwards's divine and supernatural light, or the Inner Light of the Quakers, or the exalted vision of Being in Plato and the Platonic tradition down to Coleridge. Vague and eclectic, Transcendentalism sought support not only in Kant and other Germans, but in Plato, Plotinus, the Hindu epics, and wherever the sages and the poets seemed to have touched a high reality. It differed from its New England background of Calvinism in celebrating not the omnipotence of God but the limitless possibilities of the self.

Two men of Concord perhaps offer the best way to grasp the significance of Transcendentalism, through their lives and writings. Emerson was the leader of the movement, yet gathered no disciples. The only way to follow him was, paradoxically, to go one's own way, be wholly one's self and nowise an imitator. Emerson's own way led him to resign his ministry in the Unitarian church and to seek a strictly personal religion, together with a new vocation, that of writing and lecturing to further spiritual ends. In *Nature* he condensed with at least a show of system the doctrine and aspiration of the new movement. In the address on the American Scholar he wrote our definitive declaration of cultural independence, and tried to direct the literary and ministerial class who should justify independence. In a long stream of lectures and essays on well-nigh every aspect of life, he expressed the optimism, the confident self-reliance of the young Republic, preached the limitless capacities of man, of every man no matter how common. He encouraged the United States of that day to think out the implications of the democratic slogans, and to aim at an achievement in the realm of the spirit equal to its achievement in material prosperity. In his desire to call forth the best that the self might exalt itself to, he magnified the spark of divinity that seems to touch man, till the self appeared to be God! It was only later, in essays not regarded as among the most "Emersonian," that he doubted this bold extension of romantic individualism, and limited it with a respect for actual experience and the concept of a Fate that reminds us that men are but human. On the other hand, Emerson came to feel, through faith in progress, a new source of optimism. In general we may perhaps say of him, as James T. Adams said, that "In no other author can we get so close to the whole of the American spirit as in Emerson."

An even more resolute man of Concord was Emerson's friend Thoreau. Austerely self-sufficient, non-conformist by principle and practice, he led his own life as completely as anyone could without wholly breaking away from society, as he demonstrated by his temporary hermitage at Walden Pond. He followed where the spirit led: had no other vocation, refusing to let any deadening routine interfere with his effort to keep himself fresh and alert in his relation with himself and the world. What little he needed to sustain himself, unmarried, he easily earned by doing odd jobs. He loved nature without sentimentalism, sauntered to watch the seasons and entertain thoughts, often alone, often with a companion. In his best writing he described the life of nature sensitively, and examined the values of human existence with honesty and wit. "The transcendental philosophy," he said waggishly, "needs the leaven of humor to render it light and digestible." He inveighed against low aims, stupid conventions, and the meaningless pursuit of material prosperity. The scope of thought in which

he lived is indicated well enough by an entry in his journal in
1851: "Perchance this window-seat in which we sit discoursing
Transcendentalism, with only Germany and Greece stretching
behind our minds, was made so deep because this was a few years
ago a garrison-house" of the Puritans against the Indians. Germany
and Greece represent Thoreau's concern with the European tradition, in what he considered its truest moments, from Homer
down to his own contemporaries. At the same time he made the
Puritan past of New England very real to himself, and persistently
studied the Indians, since whatever was wild in nature or man
had for him a fundamental value.

   Cambridge and Boston. Viewed from the abodes of urbanity
and scholarship in Boston and Cambridge, the Transcendentalists
looked like eccentrics. Lowell pictured Thoreau as mainly an
egotist with scant logic and no humor. And he found the group
in general, at least its faddist fringe, simply comical:

   Every form of intellectual and physical dyspepsia brought
   forth its gospel. . . . No brain but had its private maggot,
   which must have found pitiably short commons sometimes.
   Not a few impecunious zealots abjured the use of money
   (unless earned by other people), professing to live on the
   internal revenues of the spirit. Some had an assurance of
   instant millenium so soon as hooks and eyes should be substi-
   tuted for buttons. . . . Many foreign revolutionists out of
   work added to the general misunderstanding their contribution of broken English in every most ingenious form of
   fracture.

   Beside a passage like this we may extract a sentence from the
privacy of Emerson's journal, where he speaks of Longfellow in
his mansion at Cambridge. "If Socrates were here we could go and
talk with him; but Longfellow we cannot go and talk with; there
is a palace, and servants, and a row of bottles of different colored
wines, and wine glasses, and fine coats." To Concord *that* was
oddity; the appropriate thing was plain living. But in truth Longfellow had a gracious, simple nature and was no more spoiled
by affluence than the great Virginian who had made this same
"palace" his headquarters — George Washington.

   Longfellow had a wider influence on his generation, according
to Samuel E. Morison, than any other American writer save
Emerson. He domesticated for the ordinary American the courtly

muses of Europe. To a middle-class nation undernourished by the moralism of the Puritan Age and the rationalism of the next age, he brought in obvious rhythms the warmth, the color, the rich variety, the sentiment and magic, of the unfamiliar old cultures abroad, German, Spanish, Portuguese, Italian, Belgian, Scandanavian. He did this, to be sure, romantically, ignoring (as Irving had done) the living present of Europe, slighting in the past the discipline of its great illuminations, placing his emphasis rather on the picturesque, the "quaint," a realm of beauty and strangeness, a dream-world offering escape — life being "prosaic in this country to the last degree." From a prosaic present he turned not only to the European but also the American past. As he said, "The dreary old Puritanical times begin to look romantic in the distance." The moralistic twist which he gave his poems made them acceptable to a middle-class nation very definitely on the side of virtue. With that kept in view it was ready, at last, to enter the palace of art.

Longfellow, and Lowell after him, held the professorship of *belles-lettres* at Harvard. Oliver Wendell Holmes was professor of medicine and dean of the medical school. When Lowell entered Harvard as a student in 1834, there were only 220 undergraduates. According to Edward Everett Hale, "The whole drift of fashion, occupation, and habit among the undergraduates ran in lines suggested by literature." The books they bought or took from the library were works of literature — not theology, or politics, or science. "Some Philadelphia publisher had printed in one volume Coleridge's poems, Shelley's, and Keats's. . . . you saw the book pretty much everywhere."

The College was enclosed in the Yard, and the Yard was at the center of the little country town, in which old colonial houses reposed in dignity under the elms. Boston, less than an hour's walk, offered a chance to lounge in the Corner Bookstore, or hear a poem or lecture at the Odeon, or see the paintings of Allston, or watch Fanny Elssler dance. In the 1840's in Boston as in Concord, "not a cause but had its prophet" — such causes as transcendentalism, spiritualism, anti-slavery, feminism. But this was a turbulence in a stream whose main current was mercantile and socially exclusive. One foreigner after another commented upon the gracious living of Boston, a city at home with books, with talk of theology and art, a city where both family and culture counted, while wealth grew. To Holmes it was the hub of the universe.

Aside from the three academic writers of Cambridge, Boston had literati of its own. Among them was Thomas W. Parsons, a native of the city, a dentist who wrote accomplished poetry and who loved Dante as Longfellow and Lowell did, translating admirably most of the *Divine Comedy*. There was Orestes Brownson, prominent as editor of the *Democratic Review* and other quarterlies, writer of numerous books including a novel, and successively a Presbyterian, a Universalist, an independent, a Unitarian minister, and finally a Roman Catholic. There was Francis Parkman, born in Boston, still regarded as the greatest of American historians, who applied to the epic struggle of France and England in America a combination of the scientific method of German scholarship and the literary approach of Walter Scott.

Charleston. New York, Concord, Cambridge, and Boston — there was only one other place that could be called a literary center: Charleston, in the heart of the Cotton Kingdom. More obviously it was a social center, where in the winter season Charlestonian aristocrats were joined by others from all over the South, and lived a gay yet decorous life of dinners, balls, theater, races. Social applause went to leadership in politics and agriculture, not literature. Those bookishly inclined had the old classical taste, scant interest in anything new. The rest of the white population had too little schooling to give writers an adequate audience. Small wonder that Simms, the novelist, complained that all he had produced was only "poured to waste in Charleston, which has never smiled on any of my labors," or that the poet Timrod declared it to be "the firm conviction of the South that genius—literary genius, at least— is an exotic that will not flower on a Southern soil." Besides, there was slight chance for a literary blossoming in the ever more shrill excitement over slavery and the Irrepressible Conflict. Fort Sumter, in the harbor, was a portent of the fury to come.

In the face of all this, a coterie of writers did flourish, after a fashion, in the decade before the war. It had its beginnings in a group led by H. S. Legaré — a "classicist tempered by romanticism," Edd W. Parks calls him — who had founded the *Southern Review* in 1828. In all, Charleston actually had as many as sixty-three magazines between the closing years of the eighteenth century and the Civil War, most of them short-lived. After the death of Legaré, the leader was William Gilmore Simms, a native Charlestonion handicapped by his undistinguished origin but vigorous enough to become an arrogant literary dictator and to produce a vast output of magazines, novels, biographies, and verse. By 1860 he had published eighteen volumes of poetry alone, largely inspired by Byron and Wordsworth. In his many novels, such as *The Yemassee,* a historical romance of early colonial days in South Carolina, he followed the lead of Scott and especially Cooper. He gave effective encouragement to such young poets as Timrod, Hayne, and J. M. Legaré. These, with others, gathered at Russell's Bookstore to have good talk about books, to read poems, to argue over theories. In general their views were those common in the Romantic Movement, with a significant exception. Convinced defenders of the slave system and the Southern way of life, they did not share in any of the aspirations toward reform or basic renewal of society characteristic of such writers as Wordsworth and Shelley, Emerson and Lowell.

The Charleston coterie and its hopes disappeared in the war. Timrod died in 1867. He was succeeded by a late romanticist, a poet not associated with Charleston — Sidney Lanier. But Southern romanticism had already flowered at its best long before the war in the Boston-born Virginian, Poe, a tragic figure moving among the seaboard cities, Boston, New York, Philadelphia, Baltimore, essentially solitary in all of them.

THE ROMANTIC VIEW OF LIFE

The broad facts of American romanticism are now before us. Its revolt: against the rationalism that dominated the eighteenth century and lingered among the Unitarians. Its affirmation: the supremacy of the heart, the inner life of the self. Its environment: expansive, optimistic young America from about 1820 to the Civil War. Its development in literary centers: Transcendental Concord and elsewhere in the East and South, with a few of its chief writers, Poe, Melville, and Whitman, more or less apart from any group. If we have nowhere presented a set definition of romanticism, this is because its complexities have eluded all scholarly efforts to enclose it in an acceptable formula. But we cannot ignore the complexities. The significance of the literature of the period will be clearer if we make some attempt to explore and describe the romantic quest, without constantly stopping to qualify our statements. It will be clearer, too, if we frequently turn, as our writers did, to European examples.

Romantic Individualism. "Individualism in feeling and imagination" will perhaps serve as a label for the confusing elements entering into romantic literature, but only an analysis will make such a label really useful. The individualism demanded by the romantics was something other than the rational individualism of the age of Franklin and Jefferson. Jefferson had said: "Fix reason firmly in her seat, and call to her tribunal every fact, every opinion. . . . Neither believe nor reject anything because other persons . . . have rejected or believed it. Your own reason is the only oracle given you by heaven." The romantics shared this hostility to authority, but not the deference to reason. They boldly unfixed reason from her seat, and declared that the true oracle is intuition — something they knew without reasoning, something that satisfied the instincts of the heart. The individualism they proclaimed was that of the whole self, in which the affirmation of the feelings and imagination seemed to be central.

"Trust thyself: every heart vibrates to that iron string," said Emerson. He said: "If the single man plant himself indomitably on his instincts, and there abide, the huge world will come round to him." He said: "Whoso would be a man, must be a non-conformist." He said: "The root and the seed of democracy is the doctrine, Judge for yourself. Reverence thyself."

Now, self-reliance has been justified in two opposite ways — because all men are different from each other, and because they are all alike. The view that they are different has been associated with romanticism ever since Rousseau began his *Confessions* by declaring that he was made unlike anybody he had ever seen; different, if not better. All men, it seems, are born free and different, and each should be himself and pursue happiness in his own way. "Is it not the chief disgrace in the world," asked Emerson, "not to yield that peculiar fruit which each man was created to bear?" The dignity of man requires that a man insist on himself and never imitate other men. In the same vein Walt Whitman speaks of the thought that comes to us, a thought calm "like the stars, shining eternal. This is the thought of identity — yours for you, as mine for me." A man, says Whitman, has his "own central idea and purpose," grows from it and to it. While he may gather and absorb influences from outside, he must never imperil "the precious idiocrasy and special nativity and intention that he is, the man's self." This idea of the uniqueness of every man runs, as an assumption if not an assertion, all through the Romantic Movement, anticipating our modern scientific study of "individual differences."

In direct contrast is the idea of the Neo-Classic Age that all men are basically the same: not the uniqueness of men but the unity of man, not the particular man but the universal man. The two views do not, of course, exclude each other, but simply emphasize two aspects of humanity. Both views are common in this period, both the romantic sense of difference or novelty and the old Classical sense — going back to Socrates and Plato — of sameness or universality. We have quoted Emerson's doctrine of uniqueness, but actually his prevailing emphasis was on unity, though in the end he gave unity itself, as we shall see, a romantic twist. In a *Dial* paper he directly contrasted the two views, and left no doubt as to his choice of emphasis. There is, he said, a healthy subjectivism and an unhealthy subjectivism. The danger of subjectivism is shown when it is indulged by the narrow-minded and the selfish, in whom it is a form of personal vanity, or escape from inner sickness. This is the "abominable self." On the other hand, there is an impersonal subjectivism. "A man may say I, and never refer to himself as an individual. . . . The great man, even whilst he relates a private fact personal to him, is really leading us away from him to an universal experience." The reason is, "that there is One Mind, and that all the powers and privileges which lie in any, lie in all." This last quotation, it will be observed, sums up the central drift of essay after essay in Emerson's best-known writings. Thus, in *Essays, First Series,* Emerson prefixed a motto in which he says (as he wants us to say):

> I am the owner of the sphere,
> Of the seven stars and the solar year,
> Of Caesar's hand, and Plato's brain,
> Of Lord Christ's heart, and Shakespeare's strain.

Whitman later said much the same thing, beginning his "Song of Myself" with a line that looks purely personal till the second line makes it look universal:

> I celebrate myself, and sing myself,
> And what I assume you shall assume.

Harmonious though this kind of thought is with the classical tradition, it takes on, we feel, a romantic cast. Perhaps it is the focus on the ego—the inflated ego—the very notion of a "Song of Myself" in place of say Pope's "Essay on Man." Or we may say it is the bold pride of the romantic instead of the ethical moderation inculcated by a classical author like Homer or Sophocles. Or we may say, rather, that a romantic optimism, a too ready slipping into illusion, causes a certain blindness to the facts of life. In sober truth, few individuals who plant themselves indomitably on their instincts will find the huge world coming round to them. Emerson, as usual, suggests his own corrective, remarking upon the "yawning difference" "between men as they ought to be and as they are." His doubts that men have it in their power to bring into being all that is latent but buried in them, begin early in his writings and multiply and deepen as he moves on to scan the meaning of Experience, of Illusions, of Fate. He had called genius "a larger imbibing of the common heart," or "a large infusion of Deity," but his efforts to encourage and confidently call forth in every man the vast riches of humanity — to democratize genius, so to speak — were typical only of transcendentalism in its flushed heyday.

Before doubt grew upon him, Emerson accepted the view of modern philosophy, as he understood it, that "The individual is the world. . . . Every man for himself." He believed that the individual, by employing his inner powers, can create a spiritual world for himself. In the highly transcendental flights of the early book on *Nature,* he often reminds us of the German romantic outlook (as summed up by Royce on page 52, beginning "Trust your genius"). Novalis, the mystic of the German school, asserted that life is not something given us but something made by us; it is not imposed on us from without, we shape it from within. The self, as Spirit, creates its own world. This is also Emerson's assertion in the rapturous last paragraph of *Nature.* Here the individual self is conceived as having divine powers of creation. In his journal Emerson says that "God is in every man" and speaks of "the omnipotence that animates my clay." This is strong language. The God within is omnipotent, not a mere spark or breath as in the Christian tradition. Within us — "*there* is the celestial host," he says in an early sermon. He writes an essay on the Over-Soul, toward which we owe "perfect humility," but its "beatitude is all accessible to us," and "the simplest person who in his integrity worships God, becomes God." It is not surprising that such opinions gave offence to many of Emerson's Christian contemporaries. The unity of man had become the unity or identity of man and God. Each self, fully self-reliant, was divine. Not a transcendent God, or human reason, but the spiritual individual now seemed to be the measure.

It was the *feeling* individual, rather, with most romantics. Not developing their outlook, like Emerson, ministerially, they placed at the center of the self feeling and imagination. They sought every kind of experience and responded with sensuous warmth, trusting the heart wherever it led.

Feeling. Feeling — love — the heart: these were bepraised in the romantic period as reason had been in the neo-classic. For a hundred years sentimentalism, reacting against the rule of reason, had proclaimed the goodness of human nature, the virtue of the man of feeling. In the romantic triumph this sentimentalism was changed into something rich and strange. Feeling became far more genuine, complicated, and interesting. It was still at war with the eighteenth-century kind of reason: "that false secondary power," Wordsworth called it, "by which we multiply distinctions," an analytical power by which we divide vital reality till we "break down all grandeur." Feeling, a synthetic power, preserves vital reality, the meaning of things in their wholeness.

Romanticism restored to literature the emotional vitality of the Renaissance, interrupted by the long reign of neo- and pseudo-classicism. But now, in literature as in life, feeling was far more introverted and personal. It was individual joy, rapture, love, longing, regret, fear, hope, faith, enthusiasm, despair, an auto-registration of moods. These feelings were experienced with the keen sensibility and tumult of a youthful spirit — most romantics died early or became less romantic. The feeling perhaps most typical, internationally, was that of longing (in German, *Sehnsucht*), a vague longing for love, beauty, the infinite. The poetry of ancient classicism was the poetry of enjoyment, said A. W. Schlegel, and that of romanticism is the poetry of desire, a desire that can never be satisfied, an indefinite desire that must end in melancholy.

The romantic absorption in feeling is easily illustrated. There was Byron, for instance, who bore through Europe the pageant of his bleeding heart. There was Keats, haunted by shapes of beauty in myth and nature, who said in a famous letter: "I am certain of nothing but of the holiness of the heart's affections, and the truth of the imagination. . . . O for a life of sensations rather than thoughts!" There was Shelley, who aspired to an ideal Platonic realm of "love, and beauty, and delight," somtimes envisaged as a

> world far from ours,
> Where music and moonlight and feeling
> Are one.

There was Poe, with "a thirst unquenchable," "no mere appreciation of the Beauty before us — but a wild effort to reach the Beauty above." This was in verse; in his prose, on the other hand, he explored "terror, or passion, or horror, or a multitude of such other points." There was Longfellow, who called himself "a dreamer of dreams," who had drunk deeply of European romanticism, and spoke the language of the heart gently and happily, though not without an undertone of melancholy. And to name one more, a very different voice, there was Whitman, caresser of all life, even of death. "I am he that aches with love." "I know of nothing else but miracles." In his glowing acceptance of the universe Whitman reconciled all opposites. Body and soul, good and evil, man and nature, man and God — he blended them all in an emotional synthesis.

Is the romantic, then, like the sentimentalist, a man of feeling instead of a man of reason or of action? Basically, perhaps; and yet we must at once recognize a great difference. The feeling of the sentimentalist is weak and shallow; that of the romantic, stronger and deeper. The sentimentalist luxuriates in feeling for its own sake; the romantic, while he may often do this, is engaged in a quest of high truth through imagination. He believes in feeling as a value; he believes also that its value depends on an exertion of imagination. This is one of his key words, an old word which he used in a new way that has been common ever since. Before the romantic period, imagination had been synonymous with memory, a calling up of things past, or, by extension, a creation of something new by a recombination of things remembered. But now it transcended these old uses, came to be thought of as an instrument of insight into a truth above the field of the senses.

Truth, it was held, lies in feeling, but it is the imagination that finds it. The really vital meanings of human life cannot be approached by the systematic and internal operations of science, but only by an immediate emotional perception, warm flashes of intuition or imagination, a knowledge from within the human spirit.

Imagination. The concept of imagination is so important that it will be worth while to review a famous statement of it. In his preface to *Lyrical Ballads* Wordsworth announced that the object of this new departure in poetry was to take situations from common life — in which "the essential passions of the heart" are clearest — and "to throw over them a certain coloring or imagination, whereby ordinary things should be presented to the mind in an unusual aspect." That is, the poetic mind does not see nature and life prosaically, as literal fact, but throws over them (as Coleridge put it in one of his poems),

A light, a glory, a fair luminous cloud
Enveloping the earth.

How does this happen? First, something that the poet sees or experiences stirs an emotion in him. Secondly, this emotion is recollected in the tranquility of meditation, till the actual emotion has become a poetic emotion. Thirdly, this poetic emotion, now grown powerful, spontaneously overflows in expression. So far the poet. Other persons, reading the poem, have their feelings strengthened and purified. Most readers, belonging to "the poor loveless ever-anxious crowd," as Coleridge calls them, need to be awakened from "the lethargy of custom" and to see life freshly with eyes of wonder. As moonlight gives an ordinary and familiar scene or experience a new and richer meaning, so the romantic imagination, shedding the light of the human spirit, adds, says Wordsworth,

the gleam,
The light that never was, on sea or land,
The consecration and the poet's dream.

The views of the two poets are so close that we may speak of the Wordsworth-Coleridge concept of imagination. Again and again, from Bryant to Whitman, we are reminded of it in American criticism. Poe, for example, maintains that it is not the business of the poet to express passion — what we have called the "actual emotion" — but to "elevate the soul" by an image of Supernal Beauty. In an imaginative poem, he says, at every stroke of the lyre we hear a ghostly echo; in every glimpse of beauty "we catch, through long and wild vistas, dim bewildering visions of a far more ethereal beauty *beyond.*" Poetry should have the *"vagueness* of exaltation,*"* a certain wild license and *indefiniteness":* "the atmosphere of the mystic," a "breath of faëry." Poe was obviously following, in his own way, the theory as well as the practice of Coleridge and Shelley.

The romantic imagination was not equally satisfactory to all the leaders of the American movement. Lowell, especially, became highly suspicious of "cloud-castles," and called for wisdom, judgment, reason to steady and guide the poet, as in the ethical imagination of the Greeks and Shakespeare and the spiritual imagination of his beloved Dante. While he complained that Wordsworth could not see "beyond the limits of his own consciousness and experience," he held that Dante, though himself the protagonist of the *Divine Comedy,* had for his theme not a man but man, whose highest end was to "climb through every phase of human experience to that transcendental and supersensual region where the true, the good, and the beautiful blend in the white light of God." Deploring the irresponsibility to which the romantic imagination was inclined, Lowell also condemned its frequent morbidity or "liver-complaint." So did Walt Whitman, and more significantly, because the ground of his criticism was an optimism just as characteristically romantic as the pessimism he brushed aside. Of the modern tendency "to turn everything to pathos, ennui, morbidity, dissatisfaction, death," Whitman remarked abruptly: "I call this thing in our modern literature delirium tremens." Its presence in the wholesome air of the New World he attributed to the influence of the decadent Old World. "Europe, with all its glories," is "a vast abnormal ward or hysterical sick-chamber."

The German romantic critic Schlegel attributed melancholy to the Christian religion: it had made man an exile longing for his distant home. We have noted what deism, that acid solvent, did to the Christian religion. But the melancholy survived. As faith subsided and man was thrown back upon himself, the feeling of longing was left without any tangible object. As Coleridge said, "The moderns revere the infinite and affect the indefinite

as the vehicle of the infinite." Certainly the indefinite occupies a
large place in romanticism, both in the values of living and in
the means of artistic expression. Whereas mathematics had seemed
the appropriate guide for the clarity demanded by rationalism,
so now music — music as feeling rather than form — seemed the
natural language for the vague exaltation of romanticism. To the
German poet Novalis, for example, music is "an impression of
immediate assurance, an intuition, a vision of truest and most intimate life." In the same vein Poe suggested that "It is in Music,
perhaps, that the soul most clearly attains the great end for which,
when inspired by the Poetic Sentiment, it struggles — the creation
of supernal Beauty." Verse, to Poe, was "an inferior and less
capable Music." Yet it must be added that Poe, like the Concord
writers who eulogized music, and Whitman as well, had only the
scantiest understanding of the art. Only in Lanier do we come upon
a romantic who knew the discipline of music, while holding, like
Poe, that

> Man's love ascends
> To finer and diviner ends
> Than man's mere thought e'er comprehends:
>
> .   .   .   .
> Music is love in search of a word.

Like the indefinite, the remote and strange attracted the romantic imagination. " 'Tis distance lends enchantment to the view."
Perhaps no one has put so neatly the contrast between things near
when seen with merely realistic eyes and things remote when seen
by the idealizing imagination, as Emerson contrived to do in a
single sentence: "Every ship is romantic, save that we are sailing
in." But it was Poe who most deliberately cultivated the addition
of strangeness to beauty, in prose as well as verse. Attracted, as
Hawthorne was also, by the horrors and mysteries that the
"Gothic" writers of the sentimental movement had exploited so
crudely, he made them shapes of beauty, as in "The Fall of the
House of Usher." To the humdrum actual world he opposed visions of Dream-Land, the Valley of Many-Colored Grass, or
"ultimate dim Thule."

In the German school the divorce from the actual world was
carried so far that the fairy tale (*Märchen*) was esteemed by the
group as a whole and written by Tieck and Novalis. Its dream-

world seemed to offer a deeper reality — as many students of
the Freudian psychology might agree. More representative of
German romanticism, however, was its preference of past to
present — a remote native past: "Blessed be thy golden age,
Nüremberg!" Following the same impulse, Longfellow was to
find inspiration in the Middle Ages, and in the German romantic
writers as well. Irving's imagination was similarly captured by
early Spain: "It is a romantic country," he said, its romance
"chiefly derived from the brilliant regions of the East, and from
the high-minded school of Saracenic chivalry."

To some of the Transcendentalists, Asia counted far more than
did the European Middle Ages. Emerson found Asia rich in suggestions of a spiritual view of life, which he looked for, one is
tempted to add, everywhere save in the Christian tradition. Once
he came to know the sages and poets of the Orient, they were
never long absent from his writings. Thoreau's interest was more
studious. He immersed himself, as in bracing waters, in the Bhaga-
vad-Gita, the Vedas, the Vishnu Purana, the Institute of Menu.
He liked to speak of the "Scriptures of the Nations," by which
he meant "the collected Scriptures or Sacred Writings of the several nations, the Chinese, the Hindoos, the Persians, the Hebrews,
and others," which, printed together would make the true Bible.
With delight he received from an English friend the "royal gift"
of twenty-four volumes "almost exclusively relating to ancient
Hindoo literature, and scarcely one to be bought in America."
The next year, on meeting Walt Whitman, who struck him as
"wonderfully like the Orientals," he asked whether he had read
them. "No," replied Whitman, "tell me about them." And for
Whitman too the "mystic Orient" became important.

The American Past. Whatever inspiration our writers found
in foreign lands, they derived most of their subject-matter from
America — an America more or less remote. Like the Germans
they went back to the native past. A nationalistic, self-reliant
America must use what past it had. It must grow from roots in
its own soil, even though that soil was poor when compared (as by
Irving) with Europe's "storied and poetical association." To
Emerson at sea, homeward bound from the Old World, "America,
my country" was a

Land without history, . . .
No castles, no cathedrals, and no kings;

Land of the forest. . . .

Yet the mother land of our writers was not to be disowned, but prized for herself and for whatever she could offer her children. From Irving to Whitman, American writers explored their domestic heritage.

Columbus was the subject of a biography by Irving, and the Dutch of New Amsterdam were pictured in his rollicking *Knickerbocker's History* and the best of his short tales. The Puritan background became foreground in the fine art of Hawthorne's *Scarlet Letter* and of short pieces like "The Maypole of Merry Mount" and "Young Goodman Brown." In the period of the Revolution we have, among other things, the life of Washington by Irving and *The Spy* by Cooper. The Indians appear in Cooper and in Simms, in Longfellow's *Hiawatha,* in the historical writing of Parkman. Whitman gives numerous glimpses of the American past. These are only examples. Through the writers named, and others, one could reconstruct, however inadequately, the first two centuries of American experience.

While our writers in the romantic period chose to recreate much of the older America, they correspondingly slighted contemporary themes, though there were important exceptions such as Lowell's *Biglow Papers* and Melville's *Moby Dick.* They were even more aloof from the present when dealing with the European scene, making it remote in time as well as place. Thus, Irving romantically closed his eyes to the England of the Industrial Revolution, with its factories, mines, and social problems, preferring Westminster Abbey, Stratford-on-Avon, and picturesque byways. Even Emerson, shifting his focus from America and the present, wrote a book on *English Traits* and found all of his *Representative Men* in Europe.

Meanwhile, it should be added, romantic Europe reciprocally found inspiration in America, which had for it the charms of the exotic, the primitive, and the democratic. This influence in reverse has been summed up by Merle Curti. Into the catchall of European romanticism, he says,

> had gone enthusiasm for the noble savage, the mysteries of the American wilderness, the primitive in general. The cult of simplicity and the state of equality which the Americans, particularly frontiersmen and Quakers, presumably exemplified were other quarries from which

the imagination and sentiment could secure foundation stones for the Romantic structure. Thus, the picturesque, strange, and fantastic phenomena of the terrestrial paradise beyond the Atlantic gave to Romanticists the very stuff of dreams. Herder, Goethe, Chateaubriand, Byron, Wordsworth, Blake, and Coleridge, among many others, were deeply in debt to America.

Nature. To the Americans the terrestrial paradise was home. "Never need an American," said Irving, "look beyond his own country for the sublime and beautiful of natural scenery." To Irving nature was just scenery, but to our more typical romantics it was a spiritual resource valid when religion had faded, a living being (not Newton's machine) speaking to the soul in a language that feeling and imagination could understand. Nature, the near thing, was indubitably American, but the new attitude toward it came with the romantic impulse from abroad. Among the early European enthusiasts for wild nature had been Rousseau. To him nature was both a standard of simplicity and virtue and a refuge from harsh actuality. The introspective, complicated Germans went further, and fell into an ambiguity from which romanticism never quite extricated itself. On the one hand, it seemed to them, nature is a personality, a friend, let us say a divine friend, that sympathizes with man's sorrow, works upon his feelings, speaks to him of beauty, freedom, peace, happiness, touches him with intimations of high truth. On the other hand, when nature comes alive in this manner, it is really man — the poetically endowed man — who gives the life he seems to receive. Does man perhaps, as Wordsworth suggests, half create and half perceive?

However this mystery may be resolved, the essential fact, for romanticism, remains the kinship of man and nature. We strike it at once, in the opening lines of the first great poem in the American movement, Bryant's "Thanatopsis":

> To him who in the love of Nature holds
> Communion with her visible forms, she speaks
> A various language.

It was Emerson who formulated most carefully, in his book on *Nature,* the relation of the inner and outer worlds. "The lover of nature," he says, "is he whose inward and outward senses are still truly adjusted to each other." In the fields and woods he finds himself, with delight, "not alone and unacknowledged. They nod to me, and I to them." "It is certain that the power to produce this delight does not reside in nature, but in man, or in a harmony of both," though actually, as Emerson goes on, the human soul seems to be swallowing up nature, assimilating the Not Me to the Me. The harmony of the two, in his theory, depends on the relation of correspondence. "Every appearance in nature corresponds to some state of the mind." He gives familiar examples: an enraged man is a lion, a firm one is a rock, light and darkness are knowledge and ignorance. But "Every natural fact is a symbol of some spiritual fact." In *Nature* Emerson thought of all these symbols as fixed and permanent; later, as changing and transitory — so many brief illuminations. But the important thing is that correspondence meant for him what Providence had meant to his Puritan ancestors; that nature, to the sensitive human spirit, was a revelation taking the place of the Bible. Emerson might have made much of the one Puritan, Jonathan Edwards, who had glimpsed this possibility. Had he access to *Images or Shadows of Divine Things* he would have read with wide open eyes:

> Why is it not rational to suppose that the corporeal and visible world should be designedly made and constituted in analogy to the more spiritual, noble, and real world? It is certainly agreeable to what is apparently the method of God's working.

To feel kinship with nature in her gentler aspects was not difficult. One could be at home where nature invited the domesticities of hedgerow, orchard, pasture, woodlot — a more or less humanized nature. But what of wild nature? This was America's original distinction. Stretching westward from the ocean, even beyond the Father of Waters, was this "land of the forest." It powerfully affected the imagination of many of our romantic writers. Even Irving, with his face toward the Old World, remembers America's "trackless forests, where vegetation puts forth all its magnificence." "The mighty forest" dominates Bryant's "Thanatopsis," "A Forest Hymn," and other poems. Cooper gave a full picture of it: the ancient woods with soaring trees, the black mystery at night, the lakes and mountains, here and there human figures swallowed up in the landscape. Hawthorne restored the old Puritan forest, as in a famous scene of *The Scarlet Letter,* or in the sinister adventures of Young Goodman Brown "in the heart of the dark wilderness." Emerson thought of calling his first collected essays *Forest Essays,* and worshipped the pine gods in "Wood Notes."

But it was Thoreau who best communicated the tonic freedom of the forest, its wildness and beauty in large and small. In *The Maine Woods* he described a nature "savage and awful, though beautiful." *Walden* bore as a sub-title *Life in the Woods;* the life was that of wild creatures and plants as well as his own among them. To get to the heart of reality, it seemed to Thoreau, he must enter deeply into the wild. True, the inner spiritual reality was for him as for Emerson final. Yet, by the doctrine of correspondence, the inner was closely bound up with the outer reality. When the mood of wildness was on, he could "eat the brown earth," or desire to seize and devour a woodchuck raw. He loved rainstorms, and enjoyed wading in cold, bracing swamps — "a sort of baptism." As he might have put it, the Wild made him wild. But such adventures in feeling were matched by an intellectual conviction: that all civilization refers back to primitive nature and from time to time must return to its source of vitality, or decay and die. This was symbolized for him in the old fable of Romulus and Remus. The children of the Roman Empire, not being suckled by wolves, had to yield place to the northern barbarians who were. The continent of America, he goes on to say, is the she-wolf of our time. Here the moribund civilization of Europe can be reinvigorated and found a new Rome. We need not be surprised that Thoreau rejoiced when he read Whitman's "very brave and American" *Leaves of Grass:* "Though rude, and sometimes ineffectual, it is a great primitive poem — an alarum or trumpet-note ringing through the American camp."

The Common Man. With Whitman we come to one more object of romantic enthusiasm: the common man. He is the natural, earthy man. Everything, says Whitman, "comes out of the dirt — everything: everything comes out of the people, the everyday people, the people as you find them and leave them: not university people, not F.F.V. people." The People, yes the People — this has been the cry of the modern world ever since the eighteenth century. Then, as Emerson noted, such poets as Goldsmith (*The Deserted Village*), Burns ("The Cotter's Saturday

Night"), and Cowper (*The Task*) had begun to celebrate plain folk and wholesome rustic living. But it was Wordsworth who most memorably celebrated not only the natural world but the common man who lived in it, beginning with the "underprivileged" people of the *Lyrical Ballads* and rising to a climax in the shepherd poem "Michael."

In America, where the equalitarian spirit of the frontier was added to the democratic ideology inherited from the eighteenth century, writers like Bryant, Cooper, and Hawthorne were sympathetic toward the Jacksonian revolution, and Emerson (as Whitman recognized) formed a view of life basically democratic despite his patrician origin and training. No one placed a higher valuation than Emerson on the latent powers of every man: "Each man shall feel the world is his, and man shall treat with man as a sovereign state with a sovereign state." In the main he presented his thought abstractly, as the titles of his essays indicate, leaving to others a more concrete, flesh-and-blood representation. Thus, it was Whittier who gave the dignity of verse to farmers, lumbermen, and shoemakers, and who in *Snow-Bound* dwelt with loving memory upon what Emerson had called "the meaning of household life." It was Whittier also who most passionately espoused the cause of the common man made slave, though Emerson, Thoreau, Longfellow, and Lowell also took part, each in his own way.

But the cause of the common man belonged especially to Whitman. In him the currents of romantic individualism and humanitarian altruism ran strong and ran together, blending self-pride and universal sympathy. Son of a carpenter, brought up in the country and in the "village" of Brooklyn, Whitman lived his life outside the circles of gentility and learning. Common people were, for him, the "divine average," the promise of a future America leading the modern world. United in a "universal democratic comradeship," in "adhesiveness or love, that fuses, ties and aggregates, making the races comrades, and fraternizing all," they must equally possess self-pride, "a rich, luxuriant, varied personalism," "the pride and centripetal isolation of a human being in himself." With Emerson, he conceived that greatness was for each individual, waiting only to be claimed. How far he was inclined to carry romantic egoism is indicated by a notebook entry: "If I walk with Jah in Heaven and he assume to be in-

trinsically greater than I it offends me, and I shall certainly withdraw from Heaven."

Here was a poet of the people, by the people, and for the
people. Ironically, the people themselves preferred a poet like
Longfellow.

LITERARY ART

"Trust your genius." The romantics trusted it in art, as in
life. For them the essence of literary art, like the essence of living,
was self-expression.

Self-Expression. This meant a pivotal change in the concept of literature. The new concept can be made clearer by glancing back at the old. Through the ages, from Plato and Aristotle
down to Dr. Johnson, the classical mind had viewed literature as
an imitation of life, a representation of the actions of men. The
object was to picture men not as they are "actually" but as they
are "ideally." That is, a character in an epic or drama should seem
more than an actual man, for too much of such a man is personal,
local, and transient. In addition to being "himself," a character
should represent his type (the general nature of a warrior, a poet,
a man of ambition, loyalty, deceit, etc.) and, above the type,
should suggest the universal man, the ideal which human nature
is striving to attain but never actually does attain. Examples are
Hector and Odysseus, Oedipus and Antigone, Hamlet and Cor-
delia. In these extensions above the actual, the poet's imagination
is guided by reason and moral insight toward a reality higher than
the mere facts of life. It never occurs to the poet to exploit his
personal and subjective experience.

The romantics rejected this literary theory. The theory, and still
more the practice, had been distorted and diminished during the
long reign of neo- and pseudo-classicism by the development of
conventions and rules. The time seemed ripe for a fresh start. For
the old concept of literature as an *imitation* the romantics substi-
tuted the concept of literature as an *expression*. It might be the
expression of a state of society, or of a national spirit, but characteristically it was assumed to be an expression of self, of the
writer's own personality and experience in the world as he knew
it or chose to make it. Literature became largely confessional —
personal, autobiographic, lyrical. The epic, in any proper sense
of the word, disappeared. The drama was transformed, but

could not thrive in so subjective an era. Often the novel, as in Goethe's *Wilhelm Meister,* presented characters straining toward self-culture and fulfillment. The familiar essay became far more personal, as in Lamb. For the first time in the history of literature, the lyric became the typical kind of poetry. The romantic revival was indeed a period of great lyrical poetry, expressing keen and subtle sense impressions and an immense range of emotions — every variety of joy, ecstasy, of love, of yearning, of regret — with a spontaneity and intensity reminiscent of the Renaissance. Small wonder that Emerson, while aware of the Puritan in himself, exclaimed approvingly, "This writing is blood-warm." The same emphasis on self, on its adventures in the realm of the senses and feelings, appeared in the typical art of the period — music. P. H. Lang has said of Chopin, for example, that he "spoke of himself and to himself: he composed confessions."

Life and art tended, in romanticism, to be identical. Should not the poet's life be poetic, and his poetry be a living thing — himself in words? What life might be is shown not by the practical and prudential crowd, whose existence is almost a death-in-life, but by the poet, who lives creatively and freely, building his inner world of beauty and high meaning. His very life — his inner life — is a poem. And his poetry is the verbal expression of his inner life, in a word himself. Thus, the poetry of Byron is Byron, and Goethe valued it with enthusiasm as the expression of a great personality. Even Wordsworth, though far more objective, established his name by the autobiographical *Prelude* and by innumerable short pieces that recorded his personal responses to the outer world, his own perceptions, intimations, visions, moods.

This closeness to personal experience is characteristic of the poetry of Bryant, Poe, Emerson, Longfellow, and many other American writers. Our best example is Walt Whitman. Glancing backward from old age, he himself described *Leaves of Grass* as "an attempt to put a *Person,* a human being (myself, in the latter half of the Nineteenth Century, in America), freely, fully and truly on record." The book was a memorable contribution to that art of the self which is typical of the Romantic Movement. Wherein it is so different from the great books of the ages will be clear if we ask: How much of Homer is there in Homer's poetry — how much of Shakespeare in his — how much, even, of Milton in his? But Goethe was vastly more personal than these, and the

German romantics were personal on principle. It was Novalis who declared, "The novel is a life in the form of a book." And Whitman went one step further:

> Camerado, this is no book,
> Who touches this touches a man.

Organic Form. The idea that a work of literary art grows out of experience and expresses a life lived brings us to the doctrine of organic form. This favorite romantic doctrine was not new but renovated. In Greek thought we find it as early as Plato, who said that a work of art should be like a living creature. After the middle of the eighteenth century it was affirmed by Edward Young, in whose view a work of original genius "may be said to be of a vegetable nature; it grows, it is not made." Here was an idea highly appropriate to romanticism. As the universe is not a machine but a living entity, so a work of art is not a mechanical construction but an organic structure. Like A. W. Schlegel in Germany, Coleridge wrote: "The organic form is innate; it shapes, as it develops itself from within, and its fullness is one and the same with the perfection of its outward form. Such as the life is, such is the form." Mechanical form, on the other hand, is consciously imposed from the outside: "The form is mechanic when on any given material we impress a predetermined form, . . . as when to a mass of wet clay we give whatever shape we wish it to retain when hardened."

Pursuing this biological analogy, romanticism conceives of any work of art as a structure growing in an environment, developing from a living germ. Each part has its proper function, and all the parts work together as a unit. Among the parts that may enter into the complex unity and harmony of a particular work of art are diction, rhythm, image, symbol, ideas, attitude, tone, setting, character, incident, etc. Thus a successful poem, says Coleridge, offers "such delight from the *whole,* as is compatible with a distinct gratification from each component part." The parts "mutually support and explain each other." Successful poetry, in his view, cannot be written by deliberate effort; the organic principle applies to the poet as well as the poem — he is born and not made, though he can cultivate his gift.

Among American writers Emerson made the fullest use of the

organic view of art. The difference between mechanical construction and organic form, he writes in his journal,

> is the difference between the carpenter who makes
> a box, and the mother who bears a child. The box was
> all in the carpenter; but the child was not all in the
> parents. They knew no more of the child's formation
> than they did of their own. They were merely channels
> through which the child's nature flowed from quite
> another and eternal power, and the child is as much a
> wonder to them as to any.

Using the Platonic idea of inspiration, Emerson conceives that the eternal power expresses itself in the poet's intuition, and the poet's intuition expresses itself in the words and music of the poem. Spirit gives the divine hint to the poet, and the poet passes it on to all men, in a form that is excellent in proportion as it is determined by the hint itself, not arbitrarily devised by the poet. "For it is not meters, but a meter-making argument that makes a poem — a thought so passionate and alive that like the spirit of a plant or an animal it has an architecture of its own, and adorns nature with a new thing." Like all beauty, it has "fitness," a perfect adaptation of means to end. Form is not "outside embellishment" as the eighteenth century seemed to think, but already dictated by content. "A verse is not a vehicle to carry a sentence as a jewel is carried in a case: the verse must be alive, and inseparable from its contents, as the soul of man inspires and directs the body." The superior poem cannot be analyzed; you cannot separate word and thought. But in the inferior poem they fall apart, and you can distinguish between the vague thought and the awkward or conventional expression. Strictly, in the ideal poem, "There is always a right word, and every other than that is wrong." To Shakespeare writing his plays, his thought must have come with the authority of familiar truth, "as if it were already a proverb and not hereafter to become one."

Evidently the organic principle could be used to explain any aspect of creation: the man of genius, the intuition that flashed upon his inward eye, the shaping spirit of his imagination, the expression of his vision in an aesthetic order governing even the word. Not only order but disorder, according to A. W. Schlegel. Classical art, he said, reflects "a world submitted to a beautiful order," but romantic art responds to "the secret attraction to a

chaos which lies concealed in the very bosom of the ordered universe and is perpetually striving after new and marvellous births."
A paradox of romanticism was its revolt against order — though
all art has form, and form is order. Yet the wish to escape re-
straints may explain the presence in romantic art of so much that
is experimental, uneven, disproportionate, inconsistent, fragmentary, or simply careless. We might attribute romantic disorder to
the stress placed upon the values of living rather than the values of
art, which made the search for beauty a quest of the poetic life
rather than the patient and loving production of works of art.
When they did concentrate upon an artifact, the romantics were
inclined to value content more than form, despite the theory that
the two are inseparable. The wonder is that they nevertheless produced so many shapes of beauty that are contemplated with
pleasure today, notably in our own literature, *Moby Dick,* which
confronts the chaos of life with a powerful aesthetic control, and
The Scarlet Letter, in which the problem of evil is treated with
the tight economy and perfect harmony of mature art.

Tight economy and perfect harmony were deliberately chosen
as aesthetic goals in the conscious art of Poe. In this he was closer
to the classicists than the romantics. Here was one theorist who, in
contrast to Emerson and Whitman, had scant use for the organic
view of art, that form grows naturally out of idea, and at times
embraced a view almost mechanical. In theory and practice alike,
he believed that art should be rational. Yet he was not wholly a
classicist. He himself reported, in romantic terms, "My life has
been *whim* — impulse — passion — a longing for solitude — a
scorn of all things present in an earnest desire for the future." If
that was his life, his life and his art were anything but identical.
To him the natural was the rational man: "Man's chief idiosyn-
cracy being reason, it follows that his savage condition — his
condition of action *without* reason — is his *un*natural state." Writing a poem or story is a kind of action, requiring in high degree
the powers of causality, i.e., a perception of the causes needed
to produce a desired effect. Imagination is "never otherwise than
analytic." Originality is not "a mere matter of impulse or inspiration," but rather a matter of purposeful construction: "To originate
is carefully, patiently, and understandingly to combine." In his
view art is almost a mathematical logic. In many of his tales he
used mathematics or discussed its nature, and he was absorbed in

problems and puzzles of all sorts, from cryptography to plagiarism, some of which he presented in a new art form, the detective story.

The end of art, Poe holds, is pleasure. In order that pleasure may be intense, a work of art must have unity. As in the classical theory, he calls for unity of action or plot. Plot is like a building "so dependently constructed that to change the position of a single brick is to overthrow the entire fabric." Too often story writers seem to begin their stories without knowing how they are to end; they should begin at the end. When a work is complete, with a well defined beginning, middle, and end, it produces, for a few readers, the pleasure of "totality of beauty," though most readers will respond only to the intensity of the predetermined end. When plot is not the main interest, Poe invokes the romantic unity of tone, or atmosphere, as in "The Masque of the Red Death," — "*tone,* by means of which alone, an old subject, even when developed through hackneyed incidents, or thoughts, may be made to produce a fully original effect." As a strict unity of some sort is essential for intensity of pleasure, so, argues Poe, is a due brevity. A particular emotional or "psychal" excitement is created. But all excitement is transient. In fiction it cannot be sustained for more than an hour; in poetry not even that is possible.

Beauty, for Poe, is the special province of poetry. Poetry is not a mere transcript of the concrete beauties we perceive through the senses — the waving grain, the sighing night-wind, the scent of the violet — or even such interior beauties as noble thoughts or unworldly motives. It is nothing less than an aspiration in which earthly passions are transformed, an aspiration for supernal Beauty. It is not an excitement of feeling, but an "elevating excitement of the Soul," which makes all the feelings of ordinary life seem insignificant. At every stroke of the lyre, "we catch, through long and wild vistas, dim bewildering visions of a far more ethereal beauty *beyond.*"

Symbolism. Though Poe was exceptional in displaying his thought concerning external form, we may infer that most romantic writers reflected upon technical problems far more than their published works show. For example, even if some of them had little to say about symbolism, they were generally agreed that it is an invaluable artistic method for expressing a complex and difficult kind of meaning.

Through the symbol, as they conceived, the indefinite could

be suggested through a concrete representation, and the abstract thus made tangible. Instead of using familiar symbols such as the crown of monarchy and the cross of Christianity, a writer could devise fresh ones of his own choosing. Some might be made obvious to any reader; others might be left vague, stimulating the imagination to find the most fitting abstract equivalent. Symbolism is not the same as allegory. In an allegory there is a fixed and coherent system of signs, whereas a symbol can stand alone, serve a temporary purpose — a flash of illumination. It may appear once or repeatedly, and the same image may at various times represent quite different things. A good example of a symbol is the ethereal dream-maiden, in Rousseau, Novalis, Shelley, Poe, Melville.

A symbol dominates the masterpiece of Hawthorne, from title — *The Scarlet Letter* — to the very end. And as he showed in one short tale after another, his mind characteristically brooded upon or played with symbols, often with a tantalizing ambiguity. Reality, he felt, was something far too complex and uncertain to be set down in terms of reason and denotative statement. That is why Melville declared that in reading Hawthorne, "It is not the brain that can test such a man; it is only the heart."

Melville himself well exemplified his own belief that "You must have plenty of sea-room to tell the Truth in." There is plenty of sea-room in *Moby Dick,* a work that owed something to Hawthorne's deep probings, Carlyle's flashes of insight, Shakespeare's grappling with the essence of things, but mainly grew out of his own experience and speculation. Symbols irradiate the whole fable, help to bind it together. Some are used only to enlighten details of the action. The same image may symbolize quite different things in different contexts. The sea can suggest mystery, the source of life, its end, an alien element, or a friendly one. And readers interpreting with both brain and heart are by no means always agreed as to what is symbolized. Like Hawthorne, unlike most romantics, Melville was obsessed with the problem of evil in the universe. To the ship's captain with the Old Testament name of Ahab, the monstrous White Whale symbolizes "that intangible malignity which has been from the beginning; to whose dominion even the modern Christians ascribe one-half of the worlds . . . all the subtle demonisms of life and thought; all evil. . . ." Hating the inscrutable, — "be the white whale agent, or be the white whale principal," — Ahab defies the universe. "I'd strike the sun if it insulted me. . . . Who's over me?"

Poetic Style. Turning now to the question of style, in poetry and prose, we shall find relatively little on the subject in the writings of the two great innovators: Wordsworth in England and Whitman in America. Like romantic writers in general, they were more absorbed in "life values" than in "art values."

In the well-known preface to *Lyrical Ballads* the question of poetic style is mainly a matter of language and diction. As the term ballad implies, Wordsworth did not propose to abandon the long established conventions of meter and rhyme. But he attacked with vigor the neo-classic convention of a "poetic diction" apart from the diction of prose and of actual speech. He pointed out that in early times, writers, feeling powerfully, used a daring and figurative language, but that in later times (apparently the eighteenth century) they maintained this language without feeling powerfully. They used it mechanically, unconcerned about the contrast between the heightened language and their low-keyed feelings. Wordsworth gives an example from Gray:

> In vain to me the smiling mornings shine,
> And reddening Phoebus lifts his golden fire;
> The birds in vain their amorous descant join
> Or cheerful fields resume their green attire.

Such language he finds artificial and gaudy, without the urgency of genuine feeling. To restore vitality, to bring expression to real life once more, Wordsworth proposes the experiment of employing "a selection of the real language of men in a state of vivid sensation." It is not to be the language of gentlemen or of the craft of poets, but a "plainer and more emphatic language" suited to "humble and rustic life." Incidentally, he will have scant use for the personifications (Hope, Peace, and the like, with capital letters) by means of which poets had sought an easy elevation. What he wishes to do, in short, is to write like "a man speaking to men."

By the time of Emerson and Longfellow this "blood-warm" mánner of writing was common. Poetry was much closer to the currents of real life, its language more concrete, its verse freed from the stylized heroic couplet and diversified to serve many ends. Yet romanticism itself tended to form a poetic diction and style of its own, a vague and too readily flowing eloquence. We can see this style beginning in Wordsworth and Coleridge, established as a pattern by Byron and Shelley, followed in varying degrees by Bryant, Poe, Whittier, Longfellow, and Lowell. Its weaknesses are nowhere more evident than in the noble "Commemoration Ode" of Lowell in 1865. To the bold, independent mind of Walt Whitman, however, romantic verse seemed anything but an inevitable expression of modern democratic America. Rhyme for example, — "venerable and heavenly forms of chiming versification" — he regarded as fitting for the feudal order, not for the democratic.

We have already observed how Whitman felt that the genius of the United States lay "most in the common people," as he declared in his 1855 preface. The true meaning of simplicity, the "art of art," was perhaps suggested to him by the natural man, the "indescribable freshness and unconsciousness about an illiterate person." But simplicity was suggested even more, in his preface (as in the title *Leaves of Grass*), by lower orders of life: "To speak in literature with the perfect rectitude and insouciance of the movements of animals and the unimpeachableness of the sentiment of trees in the woods and grass by the roadside is the flawless triumph of art." For such simple communication he will need "new free forms" of expression: "The cleanest expression is that which finds no sphere worthy of itself and makes one." In his own poems Whitman proceeded (with hints from various sources including Biblical verse) to create a new form which came to be called free verse, avowedly if not always actually dispensing with poetic diction, personification, rhyme, stanza, and meter. He retained only the verse line, which, on the organic principle, should tally the substance expressed. The result might be called a free-and-easy, unadorned poetry, fitly illustrated by the daguerreotype used in the first edition — Walt in workingman's clothes, nonchalant and self-sufficient, "me imperturbe." Here was a poetry intended, more truly than in Wordsworth's theory, to be the natural speech of man speaking to men, an exalted conversational medium. Similar experiments were later to be made by Robert Frost, Carl Sandburg, T. S. Eliot.

Prose Style. The new view of life also brought a new way of writing prose. The prose desired by the Neo-classic Age had had the formal clarity and order of a Greek temple. Proper words were in proper places, and unity, proportion, and balance produced a design that appealed to the mind. In the Romantic Movement, on the other hand, prose had a more flowing contour, like that of romantic music, appealing to the senses and emotions. There is another significant contrast. Neo-classic prose was thought of as a *human* medium, essentially the same for all who wrote. (In practice, this implied writing with the easy dignity of eighteenth-century gentlemen.) But when emphasis was shifted from the sameness of men to their differences, it was also shifted from social communication to self-expression. Style became, consciously or unconsciously, a more *personal* medium: the mirror of a man's peculiar individuality, the echo of his uniqueness, the flavor of his special sensibility.

A good American example of what style meant under romantic auspices is offered by Thoreau. Like Poe and Hawthorne, he wrote a prose blending the old virtues of rational design and the new virtues of emotional imagery and color expressed in terms of a distinct personality. Few writers give us so strong a sense of their own essence. Prominent in the author of *Walden* are his disciplined integrity, his play of mind, his love of beauty, features of his writing that also enter into his conscious reflections on style.

Often he speaks of style in organic terms, as when he says, "It is not in man to determine what his style shall be." But this means no resting on his oars. Only by sustained effort can a man learn to write well, for "Every sentence is the result of a long probation." Mind, body, and senses, he says, must work together: "Expression is the act of a whole man." A writer needs intercourse with men and things, and especially labor with his hands, which is "the best method of removing palaver and sentimentality out of one's style." Calluses on the hands will have much to do with the writing of "tougher truth" and the firmness of his sentences. As Thoreau says finely, "A sentence should read as if its author, had he held a plow instead of a pen, could have drawn a furrow deep and straight to the end." He liked to speak with the homely reality of the farmer, being suspicious of genteel literary men and college professors, so often "weak and flimsy." With Puritan integrity and Yankee common sense he proclaims that "the one great rule of composition — and if I were a professor of rhetoric I should insist on this — is to *speak the truth.*"

Nothing is harder than perfect truth, honesty, candor, but if a writer can achieve it, "the rest will follow." Of the rest he says little, but for him, judging from his writing, it included color and warmth, surprise of the mind, a loving precision in shaping the thought, and a "concentrated and nutty" quality — his own was somewhat acrid, like an acorn. Surprise came from the use of paradox, conceits, puns, sundry kinds of wit and humor. Color and warmth came from keen senses and health, faithful observation, sensitive imagery, sympathetic response to the theme. With his reserved temperament, Thoreau generally avoided speaking directly of beauty, but it is prominent in one illuminating passage, which sums up his own notion of prose style:

> In writing, conversation should be folded many times thick. It is the height of art that, on the first perusal, plain common sense should appear; on the second, severe truth; and on a third, beauty; and, having these warrants for its depth and reality, we may then enjoy the beauty for evermore.

Both in life and in art, the extremes of romanticism were avoided in England and the United States. In these countries there was little of the extravagance, the chaos, the license of German romanticism. Though the English had largely started the movement, they were restrained, as in other periods, by their common-sense aversion to extremes and their respect for tradition. In America the strongest restraint came from the old Puritan culture, its discipline still effective even when the sanctioning beliefs had evaporated, as one can readily see in men like Emerson and Hawthorne. At the same time common sense, Anglo-Saxon and Yankee, had a sobering effect on men like Emerson, Thoreau, and Lowell. Furthermore, the romantic revolt was moderate because American rationalism and neo-classicism had been moderate, and because the way to a romantic outlook had been gradually prepared by the fluid frontier of a land of opportunity, and by the democratic revolution that preceded the French Revolution by about 20 years. The heady ideas of European romanticism came to a nation of free men accustomed to belief in human dignity and habituated to self-control no less than to self-assertion.

THE RISE OF REALISM

The Texture of Ordinary Living

❦

"Ah! poor Real Life, which I love" — HOWELLS

From the *Golden Age* to the *Gilded Age* — this is how social and cultural historians have often conceived of the change that came after the Civil War. They have looked upon the romantic period before the war as a Golden Age when farm and factory were still happily adjusted, when regional culture throve North and South, when mind and spirit flourished in an idealistic literature, and "plain living and high thinking" still had prestige. On the other hand the quarter century following the war has been viewed as a Gilded Age when the new machines of the Industrial Revolution facilitated a scramble for wealth and power, when our natural resources — farm lands, forests, and mines — were exploited and ravaged, when a continent was developed without fear of enemies beyond two broad oceans, when individualism was "rugged" and materialism unbridled and unashamed, when political and moral corruption proceeded unchecked, when science and invention seemed to point to an irresistible law of progress, when artistic and literary taste was vulgarized and debased, when, in a word, plain living and high thinking became high living and plain thinking. Perhaps this contrast has been made too sharp by a romantic esteem for the earlier period and disparagement of the later. Yet it is real enough. And it rightly suggests that the new period, in its way, is as interesting and significant as the one that preceded.

Of course the period from 1865 to 1890 was not a wholly new departure. Much that was most typical simply intensified a number of tendencies that we have already noticed in the preceding period: the spirit of nationalism, the rapid expansion of population, the invention of machines that forwarded industry, the growth of an urban and business civilization, the youthful optimism and rampant individualism, and, in the field of literature, concern with the concrete or specific and with the life of the humble. Most of these tendencies were accelerated during and after the Civil War, while to them were added new forces, such as the doctrine of evolution, the theory and practice of European realism, and folk experience as represented in homespun ballads and humor.

To the West and to the Cities

From the Mayflower to the stratocruiser, America has been the scene of restless motion. As Stephen Vincent Benét wrote in *Western Star:*

Americans are always moving on.

. . .

I think it must be something in the blood,
Perhaps it's only something in the air.

After the Civil War more Americans were moving on than in any previous period. Till the 1840's the human tide had flowed slowly, persistently, if unsteadily, westward. The ax of the pioneer rang ever a little farther in the forest, the mightiest deciduous forest in the world. But when the pioneers, pressing beyond the Mississippi and the Missouri, reached the Great Plains, vast, grassy, semi-arid spaces, the familiar woodland technique of settlement would no longer serve. The Plains were called, inaccurately, the "Great American Desert," a barrier to be traversed with a caravan of covered wagons headed for the promise of California. Many Easterners in fact preferred the route across Nicaragua or around Cape Horn. Thus the frontier had leaped from the edge of the Plains all the way to the Pacific, and by 1860 California had a population of 380,000 while Nebraska had but 28,850. Not till the 1870's did permanent settlers begin to encroach upon the Plains and Mountain regions. Then occupation grew so fast that by 1890 the American frontier, as a continuous line, ceased to exist.

But the land beyond the "Father of Waters" had not been vacant. There were 225,000 Indians — Sioux, Blackfeet, Comanche, Ute, and other tribes north and south. Peaceably inclined, they could be formidable fighters on horseback. For a quarter of a century there were constant wars, many or most of which, as President Hayes confessed, "had their origin in broken promises and acts of injustice on our part." The long, shameful story begun in the colonial East had its last chapter in the conquest of the Apaches of the Southwest. The American continent now belonged to the descendants of Europeans.

A chief grievance of the Indians was the white man's wanton destruction of the buffaloes, which had provided the tribes with food, clothing, and their principal source of money. There had been millions of buffaloes: it is said that a herd crossing the transcontinental railroad stalled a Union Pacific train for three days! In a few years they were gone, their place taken by grazing cattle. The cattle kingdom covered an area more than one-fourth of the United States. Annually vast herds were driven north from Texas to fatten on the grassy plains of Colorado, Wyoming, and even Montana. The great days of the cowboy, most colorful of all our frontier types, lasted about twenty years, while the "long drive" was possible in the wide open country. Then the ranges were fenced and the "Wild West" was gone.

To the East and the world the Wild West was typified by "Buffalo Bill." William Frederick Cody, son of an Iowa farmer, got his nickname by killing buffalo for meat, so employed by the Kansas Pacific. As a current rhyme had it:

> Buffalo Bill, Buffalo Bill,
> Never missed and never will;
> Always aims and shoots to kill,
> And the company pays his buffalo bill.

Described as "the finest figure of a man that ever sat a steed," he wore long hair to his shoulders, a mustache, and a trim goatee. He tried his hand at dime novels, such as *The Dead Shot Four,* he shot Indians in a Chicago theater, and at length worked up his Wild West Show, in which he astonished with his skill in shooting, on the gallop, tossed-up glass balls. Even with rifle bullets (rather than shot) in the first years of the show, he could shatter 87 balls out of 100. He included in his show Annie Oakley, Sitting Bull, even a preposterous feature called "Football on Horseback, between Indians and Cowboys." The show reached New York, and in England was given before Queen Victoria. Assuredly an important aspect of the life of this period is the appeal of the West to the popular imagination.

After the cattlemen came the farmers, pushing their fields farther and farther into the High Plains and the mountain valleys beyond. Farming on the plains had at length been made possible by products of the Industrial Revolution: barbed-wire fences, windmills to pump wells, railroads to transport wheat and stock to market. Yet settlers still had to cope as best they could with unfamiliar soil, blizzards, drought, dust storms, prairie fires, grasshoppers and chinch bugs — and often a load of debt. They generally came with few tools and scant furnishings, and, for lack of timber, lived in dugouts or sod houses. They endured privation and suffering, and many failed. But they kept coming. They developed a new agriculture: no longer the subsistence farm, small and self-sufficient, but the commercial farm, virtually a branch of industry, closely tied to the varying fortunes of the capitalist regime. Inventions of farm machinery came one after another, till in the 1880's labor was predominantly mechanized. One farm included in its inventory eleven gang plows, sixty-four harrows, thirty-four self-binding harvesters, etc.

The population of the most western agricultural states grew astonishingly. Between 1870 and 1890 that of Nebraska increased

eightfold, of Dakota Territory fortyfold, while a similar settlement was going on in the country of the Rockies. The number of
people living in the trans-Mississippi West as a whole, in the same
decades, advanced from 6,877,000 to 16,775,000, a gain propor-
tionately greater than that of any other section. And the center
of the national population (which rose from 38,900,000 to 63,-
000,000) had now reached the State of Indiana.

Most of the people that moved on to the Western states were
Americans of old stock, though German, Bohemian, and Scandanavian immigrants counted importantly in the upper Mississippi
Valley. Other immigrants were more likely to stay in the East. It
was a period of heavy influx from foreign lands — a total of
6,000,000 seeking a better life than they had known. The Germans were the largest group of foreign-born living in the United
States in 1890; they numbered 2,784,000. Next were the English
(and Canadians), then the Irish.

While the population was moving westward and extending the
farming land, it was moving, even more, in a second direction:
toward the cities, centers of manufacturing and commerce, which
grew apace after the victory of the industrial North over the agricultural South. New York, still easily the national metropolis, had
a population of 1,500,000 in 1870, and by 1890 added another
million, becoming larger than Paris and Berlin. Yet the most
remarkable growth occurred in Chicago, the metropolis of the
Mississippi Valley. In 1850 Chicago had only 28,000 people, but in
1870 it had 300,000 and in 1890 it had 1,000,000, having caught
up with Philadelphia. Cities west of the Appalachian crest, Pittsburgh, Cincinnati, St. Louis, and even cities on the Plains and the
West Coast — Minneapolis, Kansas City, Omaha, Denver, San
Francisco — were rapidly erecting a prosperous and comfortable
way of life. San Francisco, for example, with 50,000 people in
1860, had grown to 150,000 in 1870 and to 300,000 in 1890,
passing quickly from frontier crudities to urban amenities.

A people that had lived on or close to farms was rapidly becoming a people living in cities and among machines.

The Triumph of the Machine

After the period of canals, river traffic, and covered wagons,
came the great age of railroad construction. The railroad, with
its iron rails and steam-drawn train of cars, was naturally a pivotal

machine in the settlement and development of a continental nation. When a community was thus linked with the world, it had a
festive day. There was news for the whole world when, in 1869,
the Union Pacific and the Central Pacific were joined in the first
transcontinental route, then one of the greatest engineering feats
ever accomplished by man. By 1884 two additional lines spanned
the country, the Northern Pacific and the Santa Fe. Less spec-
tacularly, shorter roads were built in all sections. In 1830 the total
national mileage had been only 23; by 1870 it was 52,900, and
by 1890 it was 156,400.

In addition to agricultural machines, already mentioned, invention contributed to the national economy the improved Besse-
mer process, improved methods of refining oil, the steam turbine,
improved gas illumination, the incandescent lamp, the telephone,
the refrigerator car, the Mergenthaler linotype, the electric
street-car, the typewriter, the phonograph, and many other instruments of living. Whatever else modernity meant, it meant the
triumph of technology.

It also meant Pittsburgh, typical city of the new industrial
America. In two decades its population rose from 139,000 to
344,000, approximately a fourth being foreign-born. Here, where
Indians had once hunted, nature had clad in full forest green the
hills looking down upon two handsome rivers that merge into a
third, the Ohio. Here nature had also provided a region of vast
coal fields and a wealth of oil and natural gas. Factories multiplied for miles on both sides of the three rivers. Steamboats belch-
ing smoke brought great fleets of barges with raw materials, and
carried away sheet iron, steel rails, etc. down the Ohio. Freight
trains, more and more taking over the burden, pounded and
ground on both sides of the rivers, their black smoke adding to
that pouring from the mills. Then and long after, Pittsburgh was
known as the "Smoky City," with a grime that darkened buildings
and penetrated everywhere, and a sun overhead enfeebled or
blotted out. By night infernal fires flared up from the blast
furnaces, lighting the sky with a pulsating orange glow. The roar
and clatter of heavy industry could sometimes be heard for miles.
In the rush of enterprise and exploitation, the city of Carnegie,
Frick, and Schwab had small concern for natural beauty, for the
fine arts, or for the art of living. It was a city for the too-rich and
the too-poor concentrating upon material production — some-

thing very different from the Concord and Charleston of a few decades earlier.

By the early 1880's Pittsburgh had made itself the center of the nation's production of iron and steel, symbols of modern power. By 1890 the United States, forging ahead of England, was turning out a third of the entire world's output of these heavy metals. Petroleum, first discovered in 1859 in northwestern Pennsylvania, opened up a new major industry soon presided over by the Standard Oil Company. The wasteful lumber industry doubled its production. The value of manufactured articles was almost tripled, and for the first time surpassed that of agricultural crops. The Middle West, a land of farms, was becoming also a land of factories. Even the South, impoverished by the war and the loss of slave wealth, was rapidly developing manufactures. Its cotton spinning had hardly counted before the war, but by 1890 it was operating a quarter of the country's mills. By the same year the United States of America, as a manufacturing nation, attained first place in the world.

But the brilliance of American free enterprise had its dark side. The panic of 1873 started a depression in which eighty-eight railroads went into bankruptcy, nearly half the country's iron and steel plants closed down, over 47,000 commercial houses failed in five years, and masses of workers were idle and hungry. Heavy wage cuts followed, and these in turn brought on the "Great Strike" of 1877, in which property damage amounted to an estimated $10,000,000 and scores of lives were lost. Boom times as well had strikes and violence, as in 1886, when the Haymarket bomb explosion in Chicago shocked the country. The cause of labor was poorly represented by unions till in 1886 Samuel Gompers and the American Federation of Labor emerged as a force to be reckoned with. Clearly, labor was not sharing in the wealth and leisure inherent in the application of machines to natural resources. Wages for unskilled labor were less than $10 a week, often "a-dollar-a-day," and the ten-hour day prevailed — in the steel industry it was twelve hours a day in a seven-day week. A decent living, which seemed possible for all, was denied to workers. Big business was exuberantly amassing wealth and power in a laissez-faire economy, unrestrained either by the authority of government or by a sense of social responsibility.

THE GILDED AGE

Big business had been restrained before the war by the agrarian interests under the leadership of the Southern planting aristocracy. When this leadership was destroyed by the war and the horrors of "Reconstruction," Northern industrialists and financiers, finding themselves with a free hand, transformed the country with a rush, as we have seen, by the use of machines, natural resources, and labor constantly augmented by immigration — also by the use of government not to restrain but to speed up their activities (land grants, a protective tariff, etc.). In this process the capitalist class was, paradoxically enough, weaving the web of interdependence and centralization destined to be enlarged in the twentieth century, while it was following the laissez-faire philosophy that assured free opportunity to the individual. Certainly the most prominent feature of the early machine age was what came to be called rugged individualism.

Rugged individualism meant every man for himself and the devil take the hindmost. Life was a struggle for existence, a scramble for wealth and power. With many, the struggle meant a step toward the "good life" — but the good life itself would have to wait. The first step upward in the world, it seemed, must assure material success. It was not merely restlessness that drew Americans to the West and to the cities. As W. G. Pierson has put it in an article on "The Moving Americans," "lateral movement was no good without vertical movement, too." Both were included in the famous advice of Horace Greeley: "Go West, young man, and grow up with the country." To an aggressive person with an eye to the main chance, city life, East or West, offered the best opportunity to move upward. Individualism, self-reliance, was no longer understood as it had been in Concord. It now magnified Yankee canniness beyond all recognition, and dropped the old Puritan concept of a higher self to which the Transcendentalists had given new life. Or it kept merely conventional respect for Christian morals and religion, which must not get in the way of a shrewd deal. "Business is business." If a man of wealth and power, a "hero in the strife," felt the need of easing his conscience, a pleasant way was offered by philanthropic benefactions.

The rugged individualists of the Gilded Age were tough-minded men who proposed to deal with life realistically. In practice this largely meant — to borrow plain words from the historians — trickery, dishonesty, lying, bribery, stealing. A good way to understand the wild speculation and widespread moral corruption that attended the rush of exploitation is to read Mark Twain's and Charles Dudley Warner's satirical novel *The Gilded Age*. A few quotations will indicate the collusion between business men and politicians:

> Duff Brown, the great railroad contractor, . . . a very pleasant man if you were not in his way, . . . managed to get out of Congress, in appropriations, about weight for weight of gold for the stone furnished.

> [On bribery] A Congressional appropriation costs money. . . . A majority of the House committee, say $10,000 apiece — $40,000; a majority of the Senate committee, the same each — say $40,000; a little extra to one or two chairmen, [etc. etc., down to] gimcracks for Congressmen's wives and children.

> [Senator Dilworthy] He's an able man, Dilworthy, and a good man. A man has got to be good to succeed as he has. He's only been in Congress a few years, and he must be worth a million.

> [An alleged newspaper statement] We are now reminded of a note which we received from the notorious burglar Murphy, in which he finds fault with a statement of ours to the effect that he has served one term in the penitentiary and also one in the U.S. Senate. He says, "The latter statement is untrue and does me great injustice."

Sometimes the fictional representation falls short of the actual facts. Thus, *The Gilded Age* tells of "William M. Weed," said to have stolen $20,000,000 from the city of New York. But the fact, as reported by the historian James Truslow Adams, is that the Tweed Ring in Tammany Hall had in three years "carried off loot from the city treasury to an amount variously estimated from $45,000,000 to $200,000,000." How this was done may be indicated by an example. A county courthouse supposed to cost half a million actually cost sixteen times that sum. The taxpayers' money was quickly used up when chairs were listed at $470 and safes for storing papers at $400,000 apiece. Dissensions in the ring led to exposure and Tweed died in jail.

Kings of Fortune. By fair means or foul, millionaires began to abound. There were only three in the country in 1861, but before the end of the century they numbered 3800. Admiration for this new type of hero was not wholly uncritical; as Wecter pointed out, none was ever honored with the Presidency, nor had his birthplace or tomb made into a national shrine. Yet they were vastly admired, or at least envied. These magnates came to be known as "kings of fortune" (ruling the "empire of business"), or, in our own time, as tycoons, moguls, or robber barons. Nearly all had begun at the bottom of the ladder, as farm boys or office clerks or bookkeepers. The railroads had their Gould, Vanderbilt, Huntington; oil had its Rockerfeller; steel its Carnegie; finance its Cooke and Morgan; meat-packing its Armour. Merely to reprobate them as "robber barons" is misleading. While they often engaged in methods that are unethical by any high standard, they presided, with a genius for construction and organization, over the building of great railroads, the peopling of the West, the formation of large corporations, the introduction of mass production. They gave the United States the material strength which makes many immaterial goods possible.

One of the more benevolent despots was James J. Hill, of Minnesota, the railroad king who labored to fill the Northwest with people and farms. Sending his agents to the East to advertise the rich opportunities of the region, bringing Eastern farmers out to inspect the land, he caused many thousands to migrate, and transported them, with livestock and household possessions, to the localities they chose. He interested himself in their communities, in problems of farming, drainage, roads, financing, etc. His rail system, extending to the Pacific Coast, was lined with thriving farms, growing towns, and industries. And across the Pacific he explored the possibilities of markets in the Orient. On the material plane, his vision matched that of Whitman in "A Passage to India."

A very different figure is that of the financial manipulator Jim Fisk. He had had a job with a circus, then became a peddler driving through the country-side with jingling bells in a gilded cart circus-style. During the war he went to Washington, drumming up contracts for blankets. Becoming a stock-broker in New York, he soon found his natural vocation of financial swindling. In the bitter struggle for control of the Erie Railroad, he and

Jay Gould ("the Skunk of Wall Street") engaged in shameless
operations too complicated to detail here. They were summed up
at the time in the *Nation:*

> By a fraudulent over issue of stock these men had de-
> pressed the price of Erie stock . . . reaping an enormous
> profit; and with the money so obtained they had run up
> the price of gold and made another large profit; they had
> then again advanced the price of Erie . . . and made a
> larger profit than ever. In the course of these operations
> they had ruined hundreds . . . had arrested the whole
> business of the country . . . had brought the banks to the
> verge of suspension and seriously threatened the national
> credit.

Jim Fisk's malefactions were interspersed with strutting as a
colonel in the militia, as Hudson River "admiral," as producer of
operas and supporter of mistresses. He was only thirty-seven when
a rival shot him dead. Six horses drew the hearse up Fifth Avenue
preceded by hundreds of police, two bands, the Ninth Regiment,
and followed by no end of carriages and pedestrians. At the
railroad stations thousands turned out to see the funeral train as
it bore him back to his native Vermont.

In spending as in getting, the plutocracy was elaborate and
acquisitive. Unabashed by the disdainful social class that had inherited "background," it enjoyed its own version of flair, display,
grandeur. Chicago had its fashionable district, the "Gold Coast,"
and men like Potter Palmer, king of dry goods and real estate.
For his wife, whom her friends called "the Queen," Palmer
erected a royal palace, a great Gothic castle with turrets, con-
taining a Louis Quatorze salon, a Japanese room, a Moorish
music-room. But the capital city of the plutocracy was actually
New York. Here uprose a meaningless incongruity of English
castles, Italian mansions, and French châteaux. On the corner of
Fifth Avenue and 52nd Street, W. K. Vanderbilt constructed a
$3,000,000 château, greatly admired in its time, replete with
Medieval and Renaissance furniture, tapestry, and armor. With
no desire to patronize anything vitally American or contemporary,
the kings of fortune and their children turned their dwellings into
museums, despoiling the cultural treasures of the Old World.
Charles and Mary Beard, in their history of American civilization, have well described how the predatory wealthy bought their

culture: "ransacked the palaces, churches, abbeys, castles, and ateliers of Europe for statuary, paintings, pottery, rugs, and every other form of art. Even the Orient was forced to yield up graven goddesses of mercy and complacent Buddhas to decorate the buildings of men absorbed in making soap, steel rails, whisky, and cotton bagging and to please the women who spent the profits of business enterprise. . . . Mandarin coats from Peking sprawled on the pianos of magnates who knew not Ming or Manchu and perhaps could not tell whether their hired musicians were grinding out Wagner or Chopin." If it did not come into their way to read books, at least they could build private libraries of rare editions and fine bindings. Their wives spared no expense in adorning themselves: "Grand ladies, who remembered with a blush the days when they laundered the family clothes, shone idly resplendent in jewels garnered by a search of two hemispheres." There was increasing interest in the importation of family glory through genealogies and coats of arms — not always well authenticated — and through marriages of heiresses to foreign nobility.

Middle Class Taste and Morals. At the other extreme, the urban poor — far behind in the materialistic scramble — lived in ugly, flimsy tenements where dirt and disease abounded. Many immigrants who had come to the Promised Land found only squalor. Yet America's poor did not constitute a fixed proletarian class. Most of them could hope to move up. And at least they could derive help of various sorts from the public schools, the political machines, and the Catholic Church. Above such workers living in or near poverty was the large middle class, dominantly of old American stock and Protestant, merging at the top into the plutocracy. Characteristically the middle class was urban, but its traits were shared by the small town and country population. More than ever, the United States was a land of the middle class. And it was this class that gave to the Gilded Age the prevailing tone of American life, of morals and manners, of literary and artistic taste.

Middle class taste was bad, above all, in domestic architecture and interior decoration. In the building of residences, dignity was sought not through the simple stately lines of the colonial period, but through mere size and highly complicated irregularity. It was an expensive way to build, and the greater the expense the worse the result. The more pretentious residences came close to including, incongruously, everything possible: a riot of Gothic arches, classical columns, towers, cupolas, manifold gables, bay windows, stained glass windows, balconies, verandas, etc., with a profusion of hideous "gingerbread" fretwork and openwork turned out by the jigsaw. On the lawn, if there was one, often stood an iron deer or two, or perhaps Diana the huntress. Inside, the large rooms were heavy with massive furniture of black walnut, tastelessly embellished with carving — uncomfortable sofas, ugly rockers, chairs with antimacassars, whatnots loaded with bric-a-brac, tables with padded albums of family photographs, marble mantles with fancy clocks, small statues, wax flowers, and the like. At its plainer best, the middle class house could have some real dignity and grace, but the worst were excessively common.

In the middle class people who lived in such surroundings one could easily find much to admire, or to deplore. During recent decades it has been customary to ridicule them. They had a set of characteristics that came to be called "Victorian," characteristics that appeared not only in England but also on the European continent, and that prevailed most fully in the United States. Our Victorians were, in part, heirs of the Puritans; and Puritans and Victorians were dismissed in one breath in the jazz age. The middle class took pride in "respectability," i.e. a combination of moral solidity (reflected in substantial worldly possessions), a strong sense of propriety and etiquette, and fastidious modesty and reticence — to us, prudishness. Though families were large, sex was scarcely recognized. (American ladies could sympathize with the English matron who commented on a performance of *Antony and Cleopatra:* "How unlike the home life of our dear Queen!") Religion itself was often little more than respectability in formal observance, or bigoted orthodoxy without inwardness. In general there was much hypocrisy, complacency, and pomposity. With moral assurance went a practical turn of mind — a high esteem for diligence, thrift, prudence, and their material rewards. As a relief from both morals and practicality there was the easy escape of sentimentalism.

The Pursuit of Culture. Thus, while the plutocracy exploited and spent grandly, the middle class enjoyed its material solidity and moral decorum. Yet an important place was given to cultural activities. In western New York the 1870's saw the beginnings of the Chautauqua movement for adult education. At the Assembly Grounds, segregated from the world, for a summer term one could hear inspiring lectures on the humanities and sciences, and in the winters one could pursue a home reading course. Other Chautauquas bobbed up in many localities, and hundreds of thousands of middle-class Americans were soon absorbing enlightenment and enjoying good music. Meanwhile the education of the young was developed by compulsory school attendance, free textbooks, a huge increase in the number of high schools, more and more colleges public and private. The land grant colleges gave education a practical and vocational turn. Coeducation, started at Oberlin College in 1837, was widely extended in this period, and separate colleges for women were established at Vassar, Wellesley, and elsewhere. Harvard, under the leadership of Charles W. Eliot, was transformed into a modern university, and Johns Hopkins University was started as a school for graduate study only. Among the plutocracy, Andrew Carnegie had read Shakespeare when a bobbin boy in a textile factory at $1.20 a week, and while making his $350,000,000 took time out for Plato and Confucius. By founding 2800 libraries and giving 7689 organs to churches he contributed much to popular culture.

Along with this widening of cultural assimilation, was there also a creative spirit? We have already seen how, in this vibrant period, the creative spirit showed itself in business.' According to Lord Bryce's observation in 1888, business was absorbing the best brains of the country. But there were exceptionally endowed men in nearly every field of activity. Even in architecture and the arts — despite the general bad taste — the two decades attained excellence. To this day we can point with pride to the beauty of the Brooklyn Bridge, begun in 1869 and completed in 1883, the work of Roebling, a German-born engineer. In the Middle West, the sterile imitation of old European architectural styles was offset by Louis Sullivan's interest in functional form and in the use of steel and plate glass. His Wainwright Building (1890) at St. Louis is spoken of as the first skyscraper. In the art of painting, the landscapes of Inness, Martin, and Homer far surpassed those of the preceding period, despite the romantic enthusiasm for nature. In portraiture the fashionable painter of the day was Sargent, superficial but brilliant, who placed on canvas well-bred men and lovely women caught in a moment when twiddling watch-chains or flashing fans. If they had souls he did not hint, content to suggest their standard and style of living. As for the art of literature, we shall consider presently how Mark Twain, Howells, James, and others created a new movement known as realism, expressive of contemporary life and impregnated with the spirit of science.

SCIENCE AS THE MEASURE

The master key to the Gilded Age is science. It changed the scene of life, the way of life, and the life of the mind. It concerned everyone. To the man in the street it meant material progress, a dazzling succession of technical inventions that saved labor, multiplied production, reduced distances, contributed to comfort, convenience, and health, with no end in sight. Especially in the cities, all these tangible evidences of the power and value of science gave it high prestige, and strengthened material values at the expense of the spiritual values offered by traditional Christianity.

The most momentous contribution of science was the theory of organic evolution. The biology of Darwin, as basic for the late nineteenth century as the physics of Newton had been for the eighteenth, established a new intellectual climate, to which our own time is thoroughly accustomed. But to men living in the 1860's and 70's *The Origin of Species* and *The Descent of Man* presented a startling challenge. Men suddenly felt called upon to abandon the exalted concept of the human species which had been held, through the ages, by the humanistic and religious traditions. It had been clearly understood that man was specially created in the image of God, endowed with a soul or faculty of reason that marked him off from the lower animals. Now science, the new evangel, pronounced him a monkey, or a descendant of ape-like progenitors — it mattered little which! Ministers thundered denunciation of this appalling degradation of man, and laymen, even the less pious, resented the imposition of such forbears. In America as in Europe, educated and thoughtful people, though long accustomed to the general idea of evolution, were deeply disturbed when it was accounted for in purely natural terms. On the other hand, there were "free thinkers" who berated the churches for their superstition and pig-headed dogmatism. Controversy abounded for many years in addresses, books, magazines, newspapers.

Notorious among Christian believers but applauded by large audiences was Col. Robert G. Ingersoll, whose long campaign for freethinking did much to form public opinion. At Harvard a fine scientist, Agassiz, called Darwin's theory "mischievous" and never accepted it, while the botanist Gray gave it his support. One of the most effective preachers of the day, Henry Ward Beecher, also supported it. The ablest American advocate of Darwinism was John Fiske, who sought to give evolution a philosophic formulation that would allow a place for the religious principle. His *Outlines of Cosmic Philosophy Based on the Doctrine of Evolution* (1874) actually went through sixteen editions. But it was an English philosopher, Herbert Spencer, who most profoundly shaped American speculation. On the idea of evolution, or "development" from the simple to the complex, he tried to erect a complete system of philosophy, viewing man and his ideals as merely a product of nature as understood by science. With much reason, Spencer was felt to be as basically significant for his time as Locke had been for the Age of Reason and Kant for the romantic period.

Gradually the conflict between science and religion came to an end. After all, each had its own realm, and if a man chose he could live in both realms; a good Christian — Catholic or Protestant — could also be a good scientist. Yet on the whole the result of the conflict was a victory for science. Even in the more isolated rural districts, people came to think largely in terms of evolution — "the struggle for existence," "the survival of the fittest." Man was a biological creature, part of nature. Many must have thought (though few said so in print) that Darwinism had sanctioned the fierce competition of rugged individualism. Much of the public, especially the more prosperous, found a new faith in Progress, a concept vital ever since the eighteenth century and now supposedly firmly grounded in evolutionary science. People no longer sustained by the old belief in another world derived enthusiasm by believing in the glorious future of this world. Ignoring the fact that evolution, being neutral, meant only change, they assumed that it meant improvement and that progress had the authority of a natural law. Since the future is conveniently vacant one could conceive, with Herbert Spencer, that what it had in store for us was a thoroughgoing individualism, or with Karl

Marx that it would inevitably bring a thoroughgoing collectivism — though as yet Marx was only thunder on the left.

Facing the Facts. Belief in progress, to many intellectuals, was only one feature, however prominent, of a general faith in science. Dazzled by the achievements and promises of exact investigation, "pretending" (as the Beards put it) "to possess the one true key to the riddle of the universe," they made of science "a kind of dogmatic religion." This modern religion has been called *scientism,* that is, a love of verifiable truth excluding all other approaches to truth. Its scorn for the inner life was roundly expressed by a writer who began publishing late in the period, John Dewey, who said: "What is termed spiritual culture has usually been futile, with something rotten about it." Scientism rejected not only the spiritual standards of Christianity and Transcendentalism but at the same time all the constructions of systematic philosophy. As viewed by a recent philosopher, A. N. Whitehead, science itself, ever since the Renaissance, has been "predominantly an anti-rationalistic movement, based upon a naive faith. . . . Science repudiates philosophy. In other words, it has never cared to justify its faith." The intellectual portion of the public was content, like the scientists, with a mentality absorbed in number, space, time, motion, force, and the like. Even the common man, confused by the conflict between science and traditional religion, was increasingly impressed when he encountered, in newspapers, magazines, and books, the words "Science says . . ." used as if this phrase were the modern equivalent of the Biblical "and God said . . . ."

The science of the nineteenth century came like a revelation. Here, as the public mind gradually conceived, was a solid structure of proved facts in place of antiquated religious doctrines and romantic dreams. It seemed necessary to face the facts. Men have always found it hard to give their attention to more than one thing at a time. This generation focused increasingly on science— the senses — observation — facts. What could be more refreshing than objective facts, anything actual, honestly observed, substantial and trustworthy, even if not always exciting or flattering? The interesting world around us, natural and human, is full of facts. What can be more satisfying than to look at them closely, patiently? If reason was at the center of the neo-classic period, and feeling at the center of the romantic, facts came to be at the center of the realistic period.

REALISM IN LITERATURE

The aim of the nineteenth and twentieth century literary movement known as realism is the representation of the realities of life. What *are* the realities — what is most certainly real? A little reflection will remind us that this is not merely a modern question. From Homer and Aeschylus in the ancient world to the novelists and dramatists of our own time in Europe and America, writers have represented what seemed to them real, but with very different results. We have seen how, in American literature, the Puritans were overwhelmed with a supernatural reality, a personal God and Satan, a human soul; how in the neo-classic period men turned away from this conception to a faith in the high reality of a dependable human reason matching the order of nature; and how the romantics, disparaging reason, sought an ideal reality through feeling, imagination, symbolism. Now so-called realists in turn rejected the romantic vision of life as unreal, and proposed instead, as *their* conception of reality, the world of actual experience which modern science was so patiently and fruitfully exploring.

Triumphing earlier and more clearly in Europe than in America, realism was most consciously developed in France. There it arrived as early as the 1830's. The realistic prose fiction of Stendhal, Merimée, and Balzac soon led to the pessimistic realism (or naturalism) of Flaubert and Zola, and by 1885 this vigorous movement had virtually completed its course. From the critical and creative work of such writers it is not difficult to outline the characteristics of realism in contrast with those of romanticism.

Realism implies a scientific outlook upon life, sociological and psychological, instead of the artistic and poetic outlook of romanticism; it implies cool impersonality, self-effacement, instead of warm, personal feeling, confidences, confessions. Other characteristics are patient observation instead of flashes of intuition and insight; facts — detailed, documentary, verifiable — instead of guesses, dreams, visions; a materialistic instead of idealistic interpretation of life. Realism, typically, has aimed at definiteness and solidity, instead of indefiniteness and suggestiveness; the local and familiar instead of the remote and strange; contemporary life — everyday living, however humdrum or sordid — instead of the rich traditions and legends of the past. Realism has meant the use of commonplace or sub-normal characters instead of exceptional characters and the humble glorified, and it has meant the use of prose instead of verse as the prevailing medium, the novel becoming the typical form instead of the lyric. So far-reaching was this change that little was retained from the romantic regime, in the realistic theory, except keen senses, the concrete and specific, and the life of the humble.

For so bold and wide a departure from the conventions of the romantic period, American writers and especially middle-class readers were not ready. Most of the old romantic group of writers — Emerson, Longfellow, Lowell, etc. — were still active and in high esteem, and a younger generation — such writers as Bayard Taylor, R. H. Stoddard, E. C. Stedman, Thomas Bailey Aldrich — devotedly but unimportantly continued the romantic quest of beauty. The Victorian middle class, with its Puritan prejudices, still regarded the novel with suspicion, and naturally tolerated it most readily when it satisfied the standards of virtue and delicacy, as in the productions of E. P. Roe. This ministerial novelist, writing with a strong moral and religious purpose, turned out a series of novels, sentimental, didactic, melodramatic, that were immensely popular. One can guess their contents from such titles as *Barriers Burned Away, What Can She Do?, A Face Illumined, He Fell in Love with his Wife.* Sentimentally moral fiction, both serial novels and short stories, abounded in the magazines, *Harper's, Scribner's, Lippincott's, Putnam's,* largely work of women writing for women. Said the *Nation:* "Our band of heart-wrenching female dealers in false fiction was never, we think, so numerous as now." Dime novels were issued by various publishers, the most famous being those for boys written by Horatio Alger, some 135 of them, which are said to have sold close to 200,000,000 copies. As befitted the Gilded Age, the Alger books were at once materialistic and sanctimonious, picturing clean poor boys who were honest and cheerful, had a good eye for the main chance, and rose through trials to the top. The young growing up in the Gilded Age had been edified in the schools by the standard literature and pious works of the McGuffey Readers, which, according to A. M. Schlesinger, did more to influence the general literary taste and standards of the period than Emerson and all the other Concord and Cambridge authors.

Clearly, so conventional a public was in no mood to welcome a resolute and thoroughgoing realism of the French or Russian sort.

Local Color. A kind of bridge between romanticism and realism was, however, offered by writers of "local color" fiction. In novels and short stories of this kind emphasis is laid on the setting: the natural scenery, the human geography, the customs, the dress, the manners, the way of thinking, the mode of speech (often a dialect), treated in such a way as to bring out the picturesque peculiarities of a limited region. If Americans, as Henry James said, were "fond of local color," had "a hungry passion for the picturesque," it was partly because they prized regional peculiarity, when measured against the increasing standardization of life in an age of multiplying machines, seemed charmingly quaint and remote, as well as satisfyingly real. But the old provincial differences were in fact fast disappearing, vanishing in the irresistible currents of national life. The local color writer was impelled by a romantic desire to preserve a golden time when simple folk lived in happy brotherhood close to nature. At the same time he had a realistic desire to transcribe faithfully the look and feel of a region that he had lived in and understood. Thus Harriet Beecher Stowe in her preface to *Oldtown Folks* said: "I have tried to make my mind as still and passive as a looking-glass, or a mountain lake, and then to give you merely the images reflected there." Furthermore, she declared that her "studies" were "taken from real characters, real scenes, and real incidents. And some of those things in the story which may appear most romantic and like fiction are simple renderings and applications of facts."

The exploitation of natural resources that was going forward was thus matched by an exploitation of literary resources. Opening up various regions, the local color writers, with varying degrees of fidelity, achieved in terms of imaginative representation the final settlement of America, from the Atlantic to the Pacific, from Maine and Minnesota to Louisiana. In the 1870's the reading public for the first time became acquainted with a variety of native scenes and cultures. In the 1880's every American who read books and magazines was traveling, so to speak, throughout this continental nation. He could focus his attention upon New England, its attractions and oddities, in the pages of Mrs. Stowe and Miss Jewett, upon the South in Cable and Miss Murfree, upon the Pacific West in Harte, upon the Middle West in Eggleston. While the spirit in which these and other authors wrote was regional, the collective effect was national. As Eggleston said in his 1892 preface to *The Hoosier Schoolmaster*, "The taking up of life in this regional way has made our literature really national by the only process possible. The Federal nation has at length manifested a consciousness of the continental diversity of its forms of life."

As a rule the local color authors depicted life in the sympathetic and engaging manner desired by the public, romantically closing their eyes to many unpleasant facts. A remarkable exception was E. W. Howe, far in advance of his time, who wrote an acid description of the Middle West, *The Story of a Country Town*, in which the men were surly, the women fretful, nobody was happy, and "all hated each other in secret, there being much satisfaction when one of them failed." It would be hazardous, however, to assume that Howe told the truth while the typical local colorists did not: nothing is harder than to tell the truth, the whole truth, and nothing but the truth.

We can see the drift toward realism not only in local color writing but also in various folk expressions. Popular songs and ballads represented common human experience in a variety of scenes and occupations — the life of the plains, lumber camps, mines, railroads, homesteads, etc. They originated spontaneously, orally, and spread far and wide in differing versions, serving for amusement during or after work. There was also much oral storytelling, based on actual experience but embroidered. On the moving frontier there was vast delight in the shameless exaggerations of the tall tale. Hardships and hard labor were alleviated by humor. "The secret source of humor," said Mark Twain, "is not joy but sorrow; there is no humor in heaven." Professional comedians, following the homespun tradition, were highly popular: Artemus Ward, Petroleum Vesuvius Nasby, Josh Billings, and others. Their folk wisdom was often realistic in a hard-headed fashion, as when Josh Billings said, "There may cum a time when the Lion and the Lam will lie down together — i shall be az glad to see it as enny boddy — but i am still betting on the Lion." Another realistic saying of Josh Billings is virtually an expression of the spirit of science: "It ain't the things we don't know that makes such fools of us, but a whole lot of things that we know

that ain't so." In a more literary way humor abounded in the
local color fiction. Indeed, we may observe in this period inter-
relationships among folklore, humor, and local color, in a kind of
democratic earthiness. This provided a vital American foundation
for the development of a realistic movement open to foreign influences.

Mark Twain. An American democrat close to the soil — a
plain man even in his days of splendor — Mark Twain was both
humorist and local colorist. In journalism and lecturing he early
displayed a talent for lowbrow humor like that of Artemus Ward,
acquiring a lasting reputation as a "funny man." And certainly
the author of *Huckleberry Finn* and *Life on the Mississippi* was
a genius of regionalism. A regional novelist, in his view, "lays
before you ways of speech and life of a few people grouped in
one place — his own place," and novelists in other places do the
same, till in time you have "the life and the people of the whole
nation."

But Mark Twain himself rose above the limitations of both
lowbrow humor and local color, impresses us far more as an
American, an expresser of the nation. He had many traits that
Americans like to consider typically American, such as high
spirits, his plain-spokenness, his hatred of pretence, his irreverence
toward many things one is supposed to admire. Issuing from
Southern stock, briefly a Confederate soldier, this Missourian
with the wild red hair became a Westerner, but a Westerner who
spanned the nation, from California to Connecticut, in his imagination as in the course of his life.

Unlike the New Englanders of the romantic period, he threw
himself into the turbid currents of his time. Even while satirizing
the Gilded Age he could share its defects, e.g. its get-rich-quick
impulse. He used the American language of his day, the words and
rhythms of native speech, testing his manuscripts by reading
aloud. He aimed to reach the masses, he said, and he succeeded
— was and still is the most widely read great American writer.
He was not interested in trying "to help cultivate the cultivated
classes." How far he differed from the cultivated literati of the
vicinity of Boston is suggested by a Whittier birthday dinner at
which he spoke. In harmless high spirits he told the select company about three drunks in the Sierras — Emerson, Longfellow, and
Holmes. The select company listened in shocked silence, while

Mark stood there (as Howells puts it) "with his joke dead on his hands." Perhaps the failure of the joke hurt him more than the needless offense he gave. The gap between West and East was shown again, years later, when *Huckleberry Finn* was removed from the town library of Concord because Huck had chosen to "go to Hell" rather than betray his runaway Negro friend.

A mere man, Mark, in frontier style, idolized woman, the eternal feminine that draws the rude male upward — up a little bit, anyway. This led him, easygoing rationalist-realist though he was, to write a book on Joan of Arc, "by far the most extraordinary person the human race has ever produced." *The Adventures of Huckleberry Finn,* as the full title suggests, has its romantic aspect, and the realistic Huck is set off by a romantic Tom. In his great work on his cub-pilot days he showed a romantic nostalgia for the "old times on the Mississippi" (he used this for a title, later changed to *Life on the Mississippi*). Writing from fond memories, he dropped out, as De Voto reminds us, most of the sinister features of the steamboating epoch: the jerry-built — though ornate and gilded — floating palaces that invited disaster, the cutthroat, corrupt competition, the sabotage, bribery, fraud, robbery, murder, the courtesans and harlots.

Yet his conscious attitude toward romanticism was hostile. Loving actual life, he was a foe of sentimentalism, idealism, any moonshine illusion. Romantic literature — Scott, Byron, Cooper — he persistently ridiculed, with a special animus against the "pernicious" "Sir Walter disease" of the South. He showed his colors, the flag of realism, plainly in his early travel sketches. If one dates American romanticism from 1819, with the publication of Irving's *Sketch Book* recounting the worshipful musings of an American dreamer in the Old World, one may date realism from 1869, with Mark Twain's *Innocents Abroad,* recounting the irreverent observations of a fact-finding American in the Old World. For example: speaking of Florence, where the glories of the Middle Ages and Renaissance come alive to the eye, he wrote, "It is popular to admire the Arno. It is a great historical creek with four feet of water in the channel and some scows floating around." He thought of himself as a "vandal" in Europe, deflating what he saw instead of gaping like most tourists or collecting marbles and tapestries like the new rich.

He wanted to be what he called "authentic." His hearty realism is akin to that of the English humorists of the eighteenth century. He said he "had read *Tom Jones* and *Roderick Random,* and other books of that kind," and though he was nobody's disciple he reminds us often of such writers as Fielding, Smollett, Goldsmith. His masterpiece, *Huckleberry Finn,* resembles a type popular in the eighteenth century, the picaresque novel (the adventures of a rogue). In his later years his cheerful realism darkened into the pessimism of *The Mysterious Stranger,* a pessimism as black as Jonathan Swift's, though he probably owed more to a shallow American free-thinker, Bob Ingersoll. "What a shabby poor ridiculous thing man is," he concluded, "and how mistaken he is in his estimate of his character and powers and qualities and his place among the animals." But one does not go to Mark Twain for speculative profundity; he scorned philosophy, gave little thought to aesthetic theory. For the aesthetic theory of realism we may turn to his two chief contemporaries: Howells and James.

Howells and James. William Dean Howells admired deeply men as different as Mark Twain and Henry James. He wrote an essay on James and a book on *My Mark Twain.* Like Twain he came from west of the Appalachians. In his Ohio years he took part in democratic small-town life: "all had enough," he said, "and few too much." He early showed a dislike of the crude, the violent, the ugly which indicated the genial coloring his pictures of American life were to take. Geniality was encouraged, and urbanity added, when he went East — visited Boston and served as consul in Italy during the American Civil War, settled in Boston as an editor of the *Atlantic Monthly.*

Howells's early literary taste was largely classical. As a boy he wrote verse imitating Pope, and when he developed his characteristic prose style it took on, as W. F. Taylor has remarked, such neo-classic qualities as lucidity, restraint, and smoothness. His favorite English novelist was one bred in the eighteenth century, Jane Austen, whose sense of reality and of the comic in social manners seems to have fascinated him. As he reacted against the excesses of romantic idealization in the popular English and American novels, he reacted against the opposite extreme, the naturalistic degradation of man in many Continental novels. Instead he proposed ordinary actuality, a cheerful realism of the

commonplace. In his first novel, *Their Wedding Journey,* he stated
what was to prove his governing conception:

> The sincere observer of man will not desire to look
> upon his heroic or occasional phases, but will seek him
> in his habitual moods of vacancy and tiresomeness.
> To me, at any rate, he is at such times very precious;
> and I never perceive him to be so much a man and a
> brother as when I feel the pressure of his vast, natural,
> unaffected dullness. . . . Yet it is a very amusing
> world, if you do not refuse to be amused.

Howells's extended statement of his theory of realism came
much later. Removing to New York, the new literary capital of
the country, he conducted in *Harper's Magazine* "The Editor's
Study" (1886-91), from which he extracted material for a book
on *Criticism and Fiction.* Like Walt Whitman before him, he
felt that both science and democracy pointed to the value of the
common. The true realist, he asserts, "cannot look upon human
life and declare this thing or that thing unworthy of notice, any
more than the scientist can declare a fact of the material world
beneath the dignity of his inquiry." No less does democratic life as
it is lived in America invite the artist "to the study and appreciation of the common. . . . The arts must become democratic." Both
his scientific and democratic criteria ruled out romanticism, the
"mania of romanticism," which seized all Europe and caused
novelists to idealize their characters, "take the life-likeness out of
them." At the same time he saw in the texture of American life,
with its prevailing wholesomeness and decency, no justification
for adoption of the "tradition of indecency," which the French
realists had established, though he admired them on other
grounds. Life with us is not all "erotic shivers and fervors." Let
the artist "front the every-day world and catch the charm of its
work-worn, care-worn, brave, kindly face." Often Howells spoke
as if this implied a direct transcript from fact, objective in the
manner of science, without the intrusion of the author's personality
and mind, but he stated better his own full view and practice
when he called for "that sort of truth which fact precipitates after
passing through the alembic of a friendly imagination." His own
imagination, as shown in his novels, was indeed "friendly," rather
than neutral or embittered. In his view of man he took sides with
morals, and he had no desire to reject idealism altogether, long

preferring, even, to speak of "romances" rather than "novels." Whatever his insistence on observed facts, his personality was engaged.

As Howells left the West for the culturally superior East, so his friend Henry James, born in New York city, left the East, escaped from the thinness of American civilization and the crudeness of the Gilded Age, made himself at home in the denser refinements of life in Paris and London, and eventually became a British subject. At the same time his imagination always had a bearing upon his nation land. He thus found himself qualified for his special theme, the American in Europe.

In his concept of the art of fiction James owed much, at first, to Hawthorne, thereafter to English (George Eliot) and especially Continental realists (Turgenev, Flaubert). Holding aloof from much "so-called realism," he aimed at a realism leavened by ideal elements: "an ideal of joy" and "an ideal of delicacy." As a work of art a novel should not lose itself in a moral intention, and yet should show "a sense of morality" used with discretion, "as a kind of essential perfume." "Joy" suggested to him appreciation of the quality of life itself and penetration to the finest experience that life offers. What he attempted was a psychological realism, "guessing" "what goes on beneath the vast smug surface" of life as it is experienced by this and that individual. In this exploratory process he anticipated much of our latter-day science of psychology, while escaping the doctrinaire rigidity which was to handicap later psychological novelists and dramatists. He simply relied upon the artist's tools of perception, awareness, imaginative insinuation into personalities, tools that he commanded with expert subtlety and refinement. The type of personality in which the meanings and possibilities of life seemed to him most richly involved was the artist type — the writer, the painter. James thus preserved, in terms of a highly sophisticated realistic analysis, the romantic exaltation of the individual and especially the individual artist. In aesthetic sensibility he found relief from the limitations of modern society and the dilemmas of the modern mind. In respect to form, he was dissatisfied even with some of the greatest realistic fiction, such as "large loose baggy monsters" like Tolstoy's *War and Peace*. "I delight," he said in one of his prefaces, "in a deep-breathing economy and an organic form."

How could James reconcile realism, as a search for what "really" goes on in people, with the limiting effect of personality in the searcher, the individual artist? If each artist sees differently, is a valid result possible? He gave his answer to this question in a brilliant essay, a critical essay which considers the problems of "The Art of Fiction" from the artist's inside viewpoint. The writer of fiction should try "to represent life," with "beauty and truth." These are relative terms. "The province of art is all life," but the writer has only his own. Beauty must vary because art is organic: "a novel is a living thing," different from all others. And truth is not something fixed and standard, for "reality has a myriad forms." Hence the writer can properly use only the impressions arising from his own experience. He will possess an "air of reality" only when he conveys faithfully a personal impression of life. What counts above all is "the quality of the mind of the producer," his imaginative penetration, his "power to guess the unseen from the seen, to trace the implication of things." He is exactly like a painter ("his brother the painter"), for both attempt "to render the look of things, the look that conveys their meaning." Who shall say that a novel must follow a certain set of prescriptions? "There is no impression in life, no manner of seeing it and feeling it, to which the plan of the novelist may not offer a place." "There are all sorts of tastes." James's position is that of the impressionist, the relativist. He refuses to say what the artist should see, or feel, or like, requiring only that he sincerely try "to catch the color of life." James could have offered himself as an example: his ardor and expertness in pursuit of truth, especially the complicated facts of mind, equal in integrity the search of the scientist for objective truth. In James, artist and critic, realism at length reached maturity.

THE REALISTIC MOVEMENT
AND NEW DIRECTIONS

Disillusionment and the Search for Values

"A little farther into time and pain" — E. A. ROBINSON

Within sixty years of the passing of the frontier in 1890, the United States of America grew in population from 63,000,000 to 151,000,000. After the middle point in the new century it began to advance rapidly toward 200,000,000. It has become the strongest industrial nation in the world, with the highest standard of living. While strengthening government regulation, it has been wary of socialism, retaining its traditional faith in private enterprise. Its political system has functioned successfully in crises, and today it has one of the oldest governments in the world. It has a people combining an individualistic pattern of life with an immense capacity for voluntary organization; a practical people, with a large zest for production and consumption — a prevailing materialism; an idealistic people, responsive to humanitarian impulses, believing in the dignity of man and the primacy of human rights, but confused, insecure, and anxious amid the forces of a world in turbulent revolution.

Looking backward from our nuclear age, we find it hard to remember a time when American life was confidently secure and cheerful. Not in the long "cold war" with Russia, not in the frustration of the Korean War, not in the deadly struggle with Germany, Italy, and Japan, not in the longest and deepest of depressions, not in the jazz and gin epoch of the 1920's, not in the great war that broke out, incredibly, in 1914, not even in the quieter years that preceded, when the bitterness of farmers and industrial workers revealed the maladjustments left by the Gilded Age. Nor has our modern malady been restricted to the public realm of outward events. As the philosopher Santayana observed before the First World War, moral confusion has "penetrated to the mind and heart of the average individual. Never perhaps were men so like one another and so divided within themselves."

NATURALISM AND THE REVIVAL OF POETRY

Life in the Nineties. Defeated farmers headed east scrawled on their wagons: "In God we trusted, in Kansas we busted." In the West generally (and the South as well) the Gilded Age had finally brought them to despair. They could no longer endure their harsh struggle with nature, magnified by a series of drought years, and their economic plight, summed up by the phrase "10 cent corn and 10 per cent interest." For an understanding of the farmers William Dean Howells pointed to Hamlin Garland's volume of short stories, *Main-Travelled Roads,* written in a new, bitter realism. "The stories," said Howells, "are full of those gaunt, grim, sordid, pathetic, ferocious figures, whom our satirists find so easy to caricature as Hayseeds, and whose blind groping for fairer conditions is so grotesque to the newspapers and so menacing to the politicians." The menace to the politicians was real. Working outside the Republican and Democratic parties, the farm group won in 1890 four seats in the Senate and over fifty in the House. Then they organized the Populist party and two years later held a national convention at St. Louis. In a preamble to their platform they denounced the abuses of irresponsible capitalism:

> We meet in the midst of a nation brought to the verge of moral, political, and material ruin. Corruption dominates the ballot-box, the legislature, the Congress, and touches even the ermine of the bench. . . . The newspapers are largely subsidized and muzzled; public opinion silenced; business prostrated; our homes covered with mortgages; labor impoverished; and the land concentrating in the hands of the capitalists. The urban workmen are denied the right of organization for self-protection; imported pauperized labor beats down their wages; a hireling standing army, unrecognized by our laws, is established to shoot them down. . . .

Industrial workers, as this indictment indicates, were as resentful as the farmers. In 1890 there were more strikes than in any other year of the century, and in the next years came two especially alarming strikes, that in the works of Carnegie's steel company at Homestead, Pennsylvania, and that at the Pullman Palace Car Company in Illinois. The stock market collapsed, rural banks fell like leaves, wages and prices dropped with a thud, fruitless strikes multiplied, sinister fires lighted up hobo camps, "Coxey's Army" of unemployed marched from the Middle West to the national capital. The year 1894 was the darkest the United States had known since the Civil War. Small wonder that thoughtful Americans, seeing the drift of economic individualism toward class conflict and anarchy, were attracted by the promises of socialism. Socialism had a winning aspect in Edward Bellamy's *Looking Backward* (1888), which reached a sale of at least 500,-000 copies and inspired the Bellamy clubs that assailed the established order. Even the genial William Dean Howells, at fifty, took a new turn, writing a series of economic novels, hoping, like Bellamy, that democracy could peacefully introduce the principles of collectivism.

By 1896 the crisis was past. Bryan, heir of the Populist cause, was defeated in the election, Mark Hanna and McKinley were a great comfort to the bankers and manufacturers, better times arrived, and attention was shifted to the world outside. The stars and stripes had been unfurled at Honolulu three years before, and now it was time to liberate Cuba. "The taste of Empire is in the mouth of the people," said the Washington *Post,* "even as the taste of blood in the jungle." The result was a ten-weeks' war, "a splendid little war with Spain," as John Hay, Secretary of State called it. The next year we began a less splendid war with the Filipinos which roused Mark Twain's sardonic suggestion that Old Glory should have "the white stripes painted black and the stars replaced by the skull and cross bones." After an imperialist spree lasting a decade, America was to find herself owning Hawaii, Midway, Wake, Guam, Tutuila, the Philippine Islands, and Puerto Rico, holding protectorates over Cuba, Panama, and Nicaragua, and asserting a stake in the Far East.

Life in the 1890's was not, of course, all wars and industrial conflicts. There were curious or astonishing events, as when, for example, Elwood Haynes drove a horseless carriage through the streets of Chicago in 1895. At this time the bicycle craze was at its height; America was on wheels. While older people might deplore, and an eminent minister declared that "You cannot serve God and skylark on a bicycle," gay young things succumbed to the lure of the demon Speed, flashing, with tinkling bells, past the smartest horse-drawn equipages. One "got quite set up," as a diarist noted, "by passing pretty much everything, and without effort." For women there was one awkward feature — long skirts often caught in the wheels. The ideal young woman of the time, fully dressed even at the bathing resorts, was imaged in Gibson's pen and ink drawings, "a creature rather overwhelming in her perfections," as Isham, an art historian, put it, "with no occupation in life save to be adored by young athletes in tennis clothes or by disreputable foreign noblemen." Her firm chin forecast an independence that she did not yet have in that age of chaperoned innocence, an age when women cultivated domestic virtues and the arts, were expected to have what were called "accomplishments," such as doing "fancy work" with the needle, playing on the piano or singing the empty songs of the day, or making fudge on the chafing dish, or reading the light novels that avoided the serious problems of American life.

For literary taste was still romantic, well satisfied with the fiction of Marion Crawford, probably the highest paid novelist of the decade, or with that of such English novelists as Anthony Hope, whose entertaining *Prisoner of Zenda* dealt with a mythical kingdom, and George Du Maurier, whose *Trilby* told the story of an artist's model in what was to Americans far-away Paris. Written — according to Henry James — "in honor of the long leg and the twentieth year," *Trilby* was so popular in America that the St. Louis Public Library had in its stacks 400 well-worn copies. A dainty foot was called a Trilby; there were Trilby cigarettes, a Trilby restaurant, a Trilby sausage. Yet American readers could also respond, as we have seen, to a thought-provoking novel like Bellamy's picture of a socialist utopia. They could even make a best seller of a deadly serious work, *Degeneration,* by Max Nordau, a Hungarian-German who with some reason and much pseudo-scientific unreason announced that nervous exhaustion was about to bring about the collapse of Occidental civilization.

Naturalism in Fiction. But the reading public was not prepared for the plain story of an everyday instance of degeneration right around the corner — in the slums. Brought up in a brutalized environment in lower Manhattan, a girl is driven from her home by her drunken mother, works in a sweatshop, is seduced by a bartender, lives with him till abandoned, becomes a prostitute, and drowns herself. This is the story of *Maggie: A Girl of the Streets.* Clearly the novelist, Stephen Crane, had chosen to ignore those pleasant aspects of life which to Howells were typically American, and to ignore equally the popular taste for romantic make-believe exemplified by *Trilby* and *The Prisoner of Zenda.* Yet his dismal theme might have been tolerated, had Crane handled it with humanitarian sentiment or taught a moral lesson. Instead, he simply tried to tell the truth, amorally, without any judgment upon the characters' actions. The result was that he could not find a magazine editor or book publisher willing to risk such a radical departure. On borrowed money he had it privately printed in 1893. Hardly any copies were sold, and three more years elapsed before his success with his brilliantly impressionistic *Red Badge of Courage* made possible the publication of *Maggie.* In this awkward fashion a new type of realism was introduced into American literature, an advanced realism commonly called naturalism.

How did our naturalism beginning in the 1890's (as well as the earlier naturalism in Europe) differ from the mild realism of the Gilded Age? Superficially, it differed in subject-matter. A realist like Howells, for example, was generally content to hold the mirror up to the everyday life of the "good society" in which he moved. In his forty volumes, as O. W. Firkins pointed out, "Adultery is never pictured; seduction never; divorce once and sparingly (*A Modern Instance*); marriage discordant to the point of cleavage, only once and in the same novel with divorce; crime only once with any fullness." But it was precisely such "unpleasant" or "ugly" themes that the naturalists sought out and analyzed, as everyone knows who has read modern fiction or seen modern plays. Crane's *Maggie* is typical enough.

Still, unpleasant themes do not alone suffice to mark a work as naturalistic, for they have abounded in literature ever since Greek tragedy. The fundamental sign of naturalism is a certain interpretation of life, a particular philosophy. Realism, as Howells conceived of it, was as "unphilosophized as the light of common day." It wished to be in harmony with the spirit of science; it did not wish to be committed to any philosophy. But naturalism ventured to philosophize. Using scientific concepts as a basis, it assumed or declared that the forces at work in nature are in truth the only forces at work in man too. It held that the universe is completely indifferent to the preferences and desires that seem so important to us. It therefore threw out the possibility of anything in our experience that could be called peculiarly human (humanism) or supernatural (religion). Man is subject to the law of nature, and no other. He has no moral freedom to act as he chooses. "Build your own world"? Stuff and nonsense! — your world is built for you, by heredity and environment. We are all like Crane's Maggie, though perhaps more fortunate. With this biological determinism often went pessimism, the gloomiest view, as if the drift of things is always toward the worst. Nature is not only indifferent, it is hostile. Anatole France expressed the pessimistic mood when he said, "If we knew all, we could not endure life an hour."

Such are the ideas implied by a definition of naturalism in the *American College Dictionary:* "A theory, as practiced by Emile Zola, Stephen Crane and others, which applied scientific concepts and methods to such problems as plot development and characterization." Zola provided American writers with examples (such as *Nana*) and also a forthright statement of theory (*The Experimental Novel*). But the work of this French writer was only one of the forces making for naturalism in the United States. A mood favorable to such a school was a waning optimism in the face of the darkening economic and social scene, already glanced at above—the distress of the farmers and industrial laborers, the bitter conflict between the haves and the have-nots, intensified by a drawn-out depression. At the same time various intellectual influences, the acids of modernity (chief among them Darwinism), were eating into the foundations of religious and moral standards, already weakened in the Gilded Age. In literature, the older realism, having stressed the commonplace and trivial, made it easy to pass on to the unpleasant and ugly, as Garland had shown in his stories and presently showed in his critical statement, *Crumbling Idols.* Instead of conforming to the superficial popular taste, the most vital writers of this time penetrated to deeper currents and produced fiction that in varying degrees expressed a stark naturalism. Hence we have Crane's *Maggie, The Red Badge of Courage, The Open Boat;* Frank Norris's *McTeague, The Octopus, The Pit;* Jack London's *Sea Wolf, The Call of the Wild;* Mark Twain's *The Mysterious Stranger;* Theodore Dreiser's *Sister Carrie* and *Jennie Gerhardt.* In the 1890's and early 1900's romantic dreams and Victorian prettiness and evasion encountered a thoroughgoing revolt.

The naturalistic emphasis on the unpleasant also played a part in the art of painting. This was the time of the so-called "Ash Can School" of Henri, Davies, Glackens, Sloan, Luks, and others. They revolted against Art for Art's Sake, immersed themselves in the turbid currents of life, and came up with canvases, usually dismal in coloring, depicting city streets, tenements, dance halls, barrooms, prizefights, drunks, slatterns. In 1908 they defied the official art of the time by holding in New York an exhibition daily attended by hundreds, including the horrified art critics.

Meanwhile "muckrakers" were pouring into the magazines— *McClure's, Collier's, Cosmopolitan* — sensational revelations of business and government scandals, the backwash of *laissez-faire.* Some of the ablest reappeared in book form: Ida M. Tarbell's *History of the Standard Oil Company,* Lincoln Steffen's *The Shame of the Cities.* Attacks were made on every front — railroads, insurance companies, patent medicines, juvenile delinquency, the delinquency of U. S. Senators. Novelists lent a hand.

Frank Norris showed up the Southern Pacific Railroad and the wheat exchange. With fascinated abhorrence people read *The Jungle*, Upton Sinclair's novel exposing the Chicago meat packers, which caused the president, Theodore Roosevelt, to send for the author and to urge a meat-inspection bill in Congress. Yet in this same year, 1906, the heaping up of evidence of rottenness in American civilization caused Roosevelt to protest against the protesters. He called them muckrakers, deriving the word, as he explained, from a character in Bunyan's *Pilgrim's Progress* "who was offered the celestial crown for his muck-rake, but would neither look up nor regard the crown he was offered, but continued to rake the filth of the floor." Roosevelt himself, it is true, missed few chances to denounce "malefactors of great wealth," and invited Elihu Root's jibe that he imagined he had discovered the Ten Commandments. Yet his central drive was not negative but affirmative; he kept regarding the celestial crown.

Theodore Roosevelt. An affirmative political party had adopted the name Socialist in 1901, the year in which Theodore Roosevelt had fallen heir to the presidency. By the time of his election to a second term the Socialist party polled over 400,000 votes; by 1912 approximately 900,000 votes. Even this last figure, however, was less than six per cent of the total vote. Most of those attracted to socialism had in view not Marxism but some kind of socialized democracy or applied Christianity. The subject was aired in magazine articles and books and less directly by novelists, dramatists, and poets. For example, a play by Charles Rann Kennedy, *The Servant in the House*, represented a worker, Robert Smith, as saying:

> Fifteen years ago me an' my like 'adn't got a religion! By Gawd, we 'ave one now! Like to 'ear wot it is?
> *Manson. Yes.*
> *Robert.* Socialism! Funny, ain't it?
> *Manson.* I don't think so. It's mine, too.

Roosevelt despised socialism, as he despised plutocracy. Government must not own business, any more than business should own government. Gradually he took the stand suggested by the progressive movement, from the Populists to Bryan and La Follette. Whatever his vagueness and inconsistency, he succeeded in setting the pattern which Wilson followed after him, and which has continued to guide the effort of the American people to escape the extreme of laissez-faire capitalism without falling into the opposite extreme of state socialism. Into the middle-of-the-road policy he infused an ardent Americanism, which showed itself equally when he urged the conservation of national resources — soil, forests, mines — in place of the old quick exploitation, and when he "took Panama" (his own words) because he believed that the United States needed the Canal and should not be made to wait.

What America was, or aspired to be, in the early twentieth century, was well reflected in Teddy Roosevelt himself. As a contemporary Englishman observed, the two outstanding works of nature in America were Niagara Falls and President Roosevelt — what a man! Physical impressiveness he did not have, but his dynamic, magnetic personality was somehow conveyed by his tense, half closed eyes and flashing teeth, as of a carnivorous animal one had better make friends with. Fortunately *he* wanted to make friends. At the same time the Rough Rider hero of the Spanish War was always spoiling for a good fight of any sort. He carried a "big stick," called for the "Strenuous Life," despised "mollycoddles." Though he had been a sickly child, he had built himself up by sheer will power, in college was a good boxer, and in maturity had boundless energy, virility, zest for life, infectious boisterousness. He believed in America and a glorious twentieth century. He approved of all good Americans, even the wealthy. But the wealthy, to be good, must be socially responsible. Many things he himself found more interesting than making money, among them bringing up a family, governing men, fighting for reforms, hunting grizzlies in the West (Teddy bears in the toy trade) or lions in Africa, exploring the Brazilian wilderness, building up a navy, reading widely, writing history. "At Sagamore Hill (his home near New York), he said in his *Autobiography*, "we love a great many things — birds and trees and books, and all things beautiful, and horses and rifles, and children and hard work and the joy of life." Somehow he found time to write more than a dozen books, including *The History of the Naval War of 1812, The Winning of the West* (a good work in four volumes), *The New Nationalism, The Strenuous Life, African Game Trails, The Great Adventure* (on the first World War). If he did not write poetry, he took pleasure in reading it, and he served well the poetic revival that occurred in his later years when he recognized the promise of *Captain Craig and Other Poems* by Edwin Arlington Robinson and offered the poet an appointment in the New York Custom House.

The Revival of Poetry. This brings us, a long way around, to the creative renewal of poetry, a vigorous and varied outburst in the midst of an age of science and technology, of thronging skyscrapers and efficient Model-T Fords, when even philosophy (William James, John Dewey) stressed practicality. During and after the Gilded Age, it had looked as though prose was the natural vehicle for a realistic movement in harmony with the modern outlook. Poetry had seemed asleep, except for Crane's experiments, a few of Moody's poems, and the first three books of Edwin Arlington Robinson, scantly read before the revival. These were heralds of what turned out to be a fresh and vital period of American poetry, with a multiplicity of types and talents, and an impetus that carried it forward for decades.

The revival began (if one must choose a place and date) with the first number, October 1912, of *Poetry: A Magazine of Verse,* bravely published from Chicago, "Hog Butcher for the World." In the years surrounding 1912 Chicago was a focus of the literary activity of such men as Norris, Dreiser, Sinclair, Herrick, Anderson in prose, and Moody, Sandburg, Masters, Lindsay in poetry. And it had *Poetry.* This influential little magazine, originally financed by Chicago businessmen, was ably edited by Harriet Monroe with a view to giving genuine poets a chance to be heard and the public a chance to enjoy "the highest, most complete expression of truth and beauty." In its pages appeared, within the first three years, work by Ezra Pound, Hilda Doolittle, Vachel Lindsay, Amy Lowell, William Carlos Williams, John Gould Fletcher, Robert Frost, Carl Sandburg, Edna St. Vincent Millay, Wallace Stevens, Edgar Lee Masters, and Marianne Moore.

But the suddenness, volume, variety, and quality of the poetic revival can perhaps best be shown by a partial list of books of verse published within the span of only six years:

1912

Amy Lowell, *A Dome of Many-Coloured Glass*
Ezra Pound, *Ripostes*

1913

Robert Frost, *A Boy's Will*
Vachel Lindsay, *General William Booth Enters into Heaven*

1914

Robert Frost, *North of Boston*
Vachel Lindsay, *The Congo and Other Poems*
Amy Lowell, *Sword Blades and Poppy Seed*
Des Imagistes: An Anthology
James Oppenheim, *Songs for the New Age*

1915

Edgar Lee Masters, *Spoon River Anthology*
John Gould Fletcher, *Irradiations*

1916

Carl Sandburg, *Chicago Poems*
Edwin Arlington Robinson, *The Man Against the Sky*
Robert Frost, *Mountain Interval*
Ezra Pound, *Lustra*
John Gould Fletcher, *Goblins and Pagodas*
Amy Lowell, *Men, Women, and Ghosts*
Conrad Aiken, *Turns and Movies, The Jig of Forslin*

1917

Edna St. Vincent Millay, *Renascence*
Edwin Arlington Robinson, *Merlin*
Vachel Lindsay, *The Chinese Nightingale*
T. S. Eliot, *Prufrock and Other Observations*

What were the new poets trying to do? They agreed, in general, in reacting against the conventionalized romanticism of the Victorian age, which had lingered into the new century: against a poetry sweetly smooth and politely moral, the diminished legacy of Tennyson and Longfellow. They agreed in seeking fresh suggestions of technique, whether in Whitman, or French symbolism of the late nineteenth century, or English metaphysical poetry of the seventeenth century, or Oriental poetry, or the inconspicuous heritage of realistic art in such poets as Crabbe, Burns, and Cowper. Suggestions for substance, themes, attitudes came from some of these sources, and also from the fiction of the realistic movement (localism, naturalism). For a contemporary statement of the results of this reorientation we may return to Harriet Monroe, who, with Alice C. Henderson, edited an anthology of

The New Poets (1917) with an explanatory introduction. Here, despite the diversity of the new poets' methods, is a fairly accurate statement of the shift from the old poetry to the new.

To avoid the vagueness of the old poetry, the new poets sought concreteness; e.g., Amy Lowell:

> In the brown water,
> Thick and silver-sheened in the sunshine,
> Liquid and cool in the shade of the reeds,
> A pike dozed.

To avoid eloquence, rhetoric, they sought simplicity, sincerity; e.g., E. A. Robinson:

> Isaac and Archibald were two old men.
> I knew them, and I may have laughed at them
> A little; but I must have honored them,
> For they were old, and they were good to me.

To avoid wordiness, diffuseness, they sought intensiveness, concentration; e.g., Carl Sandburg in "Fog," a poem of six lines:

> The fog comes
> on little cat feet.
> It sits looking
> over the harbor and city
> on silent haunches
> and then moves on.

To avoid handed-down poetic diction, they sought the real speech of contemporary life; e.g., Sandburg:

> You tell $6 a week department store girls all they need is
> Jesus; you take a steel trust wop, dead without having
> lived, gray and shrunken at forty years of age, and you
> tell him to look at Jesus on the cross and he'll be all
> right.

(For another kind of natural speaking see the lines from Robert Frost, below.)

To avoid imposed rhythm, patterned verse, most of them sought organic rhythm, "free verse"; e.g., all the extracts above except that from Robinson.

To avoid "poetical subjects," shop-worn themes, they felt free, like the realists in prose, to deal with anything, and found most of their substance in contemporary life; e.g., Sandburg:

Drum on your drums, batter on your banjos, sob on the long
    cool winding saxaphones. Go to it, O jazzmen.
Sling your knuckles on the bottoms of the happy tin pans, let
    your trombones ooze, and go husha-husha-hush with the
    slippery sandpaper.

or Robert Frost:

> I'm going out to fetch the little calf
> That's standing by the mother. It's so young
> It totters when she licks it with her tongue.
> I sha'n't be gone long.—You come too.

Such verse — alive, vivid, natural, understandable — earned
its popularity. Once more as in the days of Tennyson and Longfellow, but in a twentieth-century way, poetry of a high order
appealed to many classes of readers. Robinson, Frost, Sandburg,
Lindsay, Millay could be enjoyed not only by "literary" people
but also housewives, lawyers, machinists, beauty parlor workers,
and truck drivers. But such widespread acceptance was denied to
the brilliant expatriates Ezra Pound and T. S. Eliot, the fore-
runners of a long list of "difficult" and "obscure" poetic artists
that flourished in the 1920's and 30's, for example Wallace
Stevens, Hart Crane, Marianne Moore, Archibald MacLeish, John
Crowe Ransom. Experimenting on lines suggested mainly by the
symbolist and metaphysical traditions, Pound and Eliot and their
associates and disciples reached only a tiny portion of the reading
public, those who welcomed the challenge of the tensely complex,
difficult, and obscure. Naturally modern poetry of this sort, like
much of the most typical modern painting and music, bewildered
and hence repelled the plain citizen.

While ordinary readers continued to think of Robinson and
Frost as the major poets, typical intellectuals came to regard T. S.
Eliot as the outstanding poetic voice of the first half of the twentieth century. He employed, in the work that established his reputation, a technique that called uncompromisingly for alert, flexible,
sensitive reading. Characteristically he offered no specific setting,
no progressive action, no progressive unfolding of logical statement. He attained form by developing a mood and attitude
through striking images and symbols linked in free association,
and by using subtly modulated repetition much as "themes" re-

appear in varying contexts in the art of music. His method was elliptical, allusive, condensed, full of overtones and hidden implications. He abounded in abrupt contrasts, often ironic, between the grand manner and the flatly colloquial, between the serious and the witty, the large and the trivial, the lovely and the repulsive.

Through an impersonal art, avoiding self-display, Eliot represented in poetic form a succession of attitudes toward the modern world, beginning in disgust and revulsion, ending in Christian faith. His earlier fame rested upon poems published in the beginning years of the 1920's. With history and myth as a backdrop, he pictured the contemporary disintegration of faith, the dissolving of tradition — a sterile waste land with memories but no hope, an "immense panorama of futility and anarchy." Human life as lived in our modern urban civilization — in London, his adopted home, as in his ancestral Boston — seemed devoid of all meaning and value. The "Lost Generation" who had survived what seemed a fruitless world war found in him a spokesman of their revolt and despair.

A DISILLUSIONED GENERATION

Good-by to World Affairs. The revolt of the Roaring Twenties had been forming since about 1890, especially in the years just preceding the world war. But the war brought on a fresh access of disillusionment. To most Americans the outbreak of the conflict in 1914 had been simply incredible. Ignorant of European history and geography, many read eagerly the explanations offered by journalists and even the background works of historians (e.g. *Europe Since 1815*). Fatefully, the American people drifted into the vortex, repeating the slogans: "The world must be made safe for democracy," "A war to end war." After a vast mobilization of physical force and moral energy under the leadership of Woodrow Wilson, the nation embarked on the Great Crusade. Surely, when the Huns had been crushed, a new and better world would be built. Nothing would be as it had been.

But when the dizzy enthusiasm of victory subsided, reaction set in. The Great War soon began to look like a Great Interruption. Then, when the "four old men" at Versailles had finished their work, it looked like a Great Mistake. The utopian slogans of the war, apparently forgotten in the peace, now had a bitterly ironic ring. America had been defeated, it seemed, by its French and English allies. In any case it had had enough of world politics, and feared the consequences of binding its future to a League of Nations. In vain did President Wilson declare to the American people as well as to the Senate, "We cannot turn back. We can only go forward, with lifted eyes and freshened spirit, to follow the vision." The vision was gone. The postwar generation, said Harold Stearns in 1920, no longer believed "a word about the ostensible aims for which the war was waged." Dos Passos in his novel *Three Soldiers* (1923) wrote: "So was civilization nothing but a vast edifice of sham, and the war, instead of its crumbling, was its fullest and most ultimate expression." Hemingway, in *A Farewell to Arms* (1929) wrote: "I was always embarrassed by the words *sacred, glorious,* and *sacrifice* and the expression *in vain.* We had heard them, sometimes standing in the rain almost out of earshot, so that only the shouted words came through, and had read them, on proclamations that were slapped up by bill-posters over other proclamations, now for a long time, and I had seen nothing sacred, and the things that were glorious had no glory and the sacrifices were like the stockyards at Chicago if nothing was done with the meat except to bury it."

Leaving Europe to "stew in its own juice," the United States pursued with zest the course of isolation. Aloof from the turmoil, deprivation, fear and hate overseas, it was pleased to withdraw into itself. A leading feature of the entire decade was the intensification of nationalism, commonly known as "Americanism," an attitude and program that went far beyond anything that Theodore Roosevelt had contemplated. It brought one result clearly enough in the national interest, the restriction of immigration. In the century between 1820 and 1920, immigrants admitted had reached a grand total of about 34,000,000, and of these, 13,000,000 had arrived in the first fifteen years of the new century, increasingly of types not easily assimilated. A quota system was devised to prevent a sudden influx from postwar Europe. But along with national prudence went sheer intolerance. The peace continued the wartime hysteria expressed in the now amazing words of Walter H. Page, U. S. Ambassador to Great Britain, "We Americans have got to . . . hang our Irish agitators and shoot our hyphenates and bring up our children with reverence for English history and in the awe of English literature."

Aliens who might have radical notions were deported by the thousand. Teachers were compelled to take loyalty oaths. History textbooks had to be revised to suit the American Legion and the D.A.R. Legislatures were purged of socialists. Military training in state schools was made compulsory. Pacifists were persecuted. The Ku Klux Klan, numbering its membership by millions, spread fear among Catholics, Negroes, Jews, and radicals. (This was its way of forwarding what it called in its constitution "pure Americanism.") For two or three years after the war Bolshevik Russia replaced Germany as the villain, and during the "Red Scare" any shade of radicalism was looked upon as a menace. The vice-president of the United States expressed alarm when the girl debaters of Radcliffe College dared to uphold the affirmative in an intercollegiate debate on the topic, "Resolved, that the recognition of labor unions by employers is essential to successful collective bargaining."

Not even science escaped the hysterical backwash of the war. Three states — Tennessee, Mississippi, and Arkansas — tried to abolish the idea of evolution, passing laws that forbade teaching, in any public school or college, "that man has descended from a lower order of animals." Fundamentalist obscurantism was soon dramatized in Dayton, Tennessee, by a "monkey trial" which became a national show. Clarence Darrow, a famous lawyer, defended the young teacher Scopes, while William Jennings Bryan endeavored — in his own passionate words — "to protect the word of God against the greatest atheist and agnostic in the United States."

Right behavior as well as right thinking was sought by legislation. State after state had gone "dry" before the World War, largely through the zeal of Methodist and other church groups, largely also through the concern of employers for the efficiency and safety of labor in the use of modern machinery. The war added a fresh motive: the saving of grain. In 1917 Congress, habituated to drastic measures, submitted the Prohibition Amendment to the states, and in 1920 a "bone-dry" law went into effect, at the very time when the country was in a mood for a spree. The twelve years that followed witnessed the flourishing of bootleggers, rumrunners, hijackers, gangsters (like Al Capone in his armored car), speak-easies, cocktail parties, and the hip-flask. While the national consumption of liquor was probably reduced, it was increased among the prosperous classes, and evasion of the law contributed much to the postwar relaxation of morals and manners.

The Big Boom. Self absorbed and intolerant, a majority of Americans smugly relished the kind of opinion voiced editorially in the *Ladies Home Journal:* "There is only one first-class civilization in the world today. It is right here in the United States." A different opinion was held by a group of thirty intellectuals (Harold Stearns, Robert M. Lovett, Lewis Mumford, among others) in their symposium on *Civilization in the United States.* They found failure written large in every department of the national life, except perhaps science. But to those content to measure a nation by its material success, America plainly led the world. There could be no disillusionment about *this.*

The great interruption over, President Harding, addressing an audience of business men, assured them that his administration favored "not nostrums but normalcy." This meant: not an adventure in an alien league of nations, nor any silly socialist ideas imported from Russia, but a return to the good old ways of free enterprise. And free enterprise meant, not Woodrow Wilson's "New Freedom" for the small folk, but the old freedom for big business, the "robust Republicanism" of the Hanna-McKinley school. The policy was continued by President Coolidge, who sagely observed, "The business of the United States is business." After a mild recession the Big Boom started. By 1926 Stuart Chase was able to report that the United States was the economic and financial center of the world. "While Europe staggers and reels," he wrote, "national America is, beyond peradventure, the Eighth Wonder, and subject to the awe and the envy which all wonders command." With lyrical enthusiasm he spread out the statistics, like a miser counting his gold. The Age of the Machine was indeed in full career. Mechanical energy gave us the equivalent, as engineers were saying, of the labor of 3,000,000,000 slaves, or 30 for every man, woman, and child in the land. Around the middle of the decade there was, appropriately enough, a popular demand for the election of Henry Ford as President of the United States. Aided by mass production, high wages, blatant advertising, and installment purchasing, getting and spending vastly exceeded the extravagance of the Gilded Age. As the flood of prosperity rushed toward the Niagara of 1929, economists and business men were jubilantly announcing that henceforth prosperity would be permanent, perhaps ever-increasing.

For two years the nation's best-selling non-fiction book was one by Bruce Barton entitled *The Man Nobody Knows:* i.e. Jesus, "the founder of modern business," a great executive and advertiser who stood for "service." While professing to serve the country, business men and politicians were freely helping themselves, as they showed by their corruption and maladministration during the Harding regime, most flagrantly in, the Teapot Dome and other oil scandals. When these scandals were exposed, the public was profoundly apathetic. Was it not unpatriotic to "rock the boat" of prosperity? Were not those who called for a searching investigation "nothing better than Bolsheviki"?

It was an urban prosperity. The farmers — the lush war years over — received only 15 per cent of the national income. The rural population of the United States, in 1920, was for the first time outnumbered by the urban. The persistent drift to the cities, by migration from the farms as well as from abroad, had produced rapidly growing centers of industry and commerce from coast to coast. New York's population of 2,500,000 in 1890 had by 1930 reached about 7,000,000; Chicago's 1,000,000 had grown to 3,376,000; and a great city had appeared on the Pacific — Los Angeles, mushrooming in the same period from 50,000 to 1,238,000. But while the cities grew and prospered, the distribution of America's wealth was fantastic. A fifth of the nation's families had incomes of less than $1000, and the richest 0.1 per cent had about the same total income as the poorest 42 per cent. Millionaires were common, multimillionaires increased, and there were billionaires. Still, even the average man had a higher standard of living than before.

The Jazz Age. The average man had access to the new means of convenience and pleasure pouring from the factories of the Machine Age. A "car for the masses," achieved by Henry Ford, was in 1924 priced only $290. Three years later the fifteenth million Tin Lizzy left the assembly line and sputtered efficiently in town and country. The automobile added immeasurably to the mobility of the American people, to standardized ways of living, to the subordination of the home to outside interests. Second only to the automobile, in altering habits of living and the tone of living, was the motion picture. In *Middletown*, the Lynds' study of a typical small city, we are informed that attendance reached, in one month of 1923, four and a half times the total population. To a people avid for entertainment the pictures offered, in the words of a *Saturday Evening Post* advertisement, "all the adventure, all the romance, all the excitement you lack in your daily life. If only for an afternoon or an evening — escape!" Who did not lose himself in Charlie Chaplin, Douglas Fairbanks, Theda Bara, Clara Bow, Rudolph Valentino? A third means of popular entertainment by machine came in 1920, when the first regular broadcasting station, KDKA, went on the air at Pittsburgh. By 1922 radio was a new craze, and the sales mounted from 60 million dollars in that year to over 842 in 1929. Life at home could now become, by the magic of a switch, the life of all America: a political convention, a philharmonic concert, a sermon by Dr. Fosdick, the crooning of Rudy Vallee. Dubiously, Willa Cather observed in 1921, "We have music by machines, we travel by machines — the American people are so submerged in them that sometimes I think they can only be made to laugh and cry by machinery."

Organized sport became a passion and a major industry. Prize fights, once outlawed, drew vast crowds, who, in two contests in which Dempsey fought, paid $4,545,000. Football came to be played in what Coach Stagg called "lunar craters," sometimes filled, says one historian, with the largest crowds of the sort since the fall of Rome. Charges of bribe-taking by the White Sox occasioned far more popular excitement than did charges of bribe-taking by members of the President's cabinet in Washington. Indoors, card-playing, once widely frowned upon, was possible even on Sundays, without drawn window curtains, and the game of bridge was all the rage. But on the whole the most typical form of pleasure-seeking was dancing.

The tango and the turkey trot had come in before the war, and they were followed by the Charleston and black bottom, a far cry from the sedate waltz and two-step of the turn of the century. According to a sober estimate, 30,000,000 Americans danced daily, weekly, or frequently. The new music, introduced about 1915, had "the syncopated rhythm of the jungle," with "pulsating groans, long wails, and fitful shrieks," and "seemed a counterpart of the cacophonous uproar of manufacturing industries and urban life" — the Beards' description serves to sug-

gest how older people heard it, though other older people enjoyed dancing to jazz and matched, or tried to match, the behavior
of the young.

Perhaps the dominating symbol of the decade was the flapper.
While women were enjoying enlarged economic opportunities and
securing political rights (Woman Suffrage Amendment, 1920),
the flapper played a leading role in a revolution of morals and
manners. A young bird flapping her new-found wings, she im-
petuously proved her unconventional sophistication. She bobbed
her hair, swore like a boy, smoked cigarettes, took to gin and
corn and got drunk ("blotto"), made the most, or least, of the
short skirts (they went up like the stock market, reached the
knee in 1927), and often rolled her stockings on the calf. Like
unmentionable women in an earlier time, she had, in her armory,
powder, rouge, and lipstick. Outrageously, she spoke whatever
came into her head. *He*: How many Commandments are there?"
She: "Ten." *He*: "Suppose you were to break one of them?" *She*
(*hopefully*): "There'd be nine."

The best account of Flaming Youth is Fitzgerald's novel *This
Side of Paradise,* though it was published at the threshold of the
decade of whoopee. Rosalind, nineteen and beautiful like all flappers, "once told a roomful of her mother's friends that the only
excuse for women was the necessity for a disturbing element
among men." "None of the Victorian mothers—and most of the
mothers were Victorians — had any idea how casually their
daughters were accustomed to being kissed. 'Servant-girls are that
way,' says Mrs. Huston-Carmelite to her popular daughter."
"Amory found it rather fascinating to feel that any popular girl
he met before eight he might quite possibly kiss before twelve."
(Five minutes sufficed when he met Rosalind.) At the end of the
novel, playing with the idea of socialism, Amory sums up: "I'm
restless. My whole generation is restless," and, having returned
to Princeton, he contemplates a new generation of students, "dedicated more than the last to the fear of poverty and the worship
of success; grown up to find all Gods dead, all wars fought, all
faiths in man shaken."

In their disillusionment, in their carnival of sex, dancing, jazz,
and alcohol, the young and their elders tried to justify their behavior by the "New Psychology," especially the theory of the
great Viennese psychoanalyst, Sigmund Freud. His name came

to suggest the lowdown on human nature and a sanction for doing what one pleases. Attention was once more directed upon the inner life — this time not the Christian soul or the romantic ego but a subconscious activity dominated by sex. In life and in literature sex became an obsession; the repression of the nineteenth century became the expression of the twentieth, the old reticence became the new outspokenness, the former discussions of religion were replaced by chatter about sex. Typical enough is the brash girl in Fitzgerald's novel who says to the young hero: "Oh, just one person in fifty has any glimmer of what sex is. I'm hipped on Freud and all that. . . ." Few people bothered to read Freud's works, but his scientific ideas were in the air. In the glib columns of the daily press, in the patter of the dinner table and drinking sessions, the technical words of the new gospel were familiarly used and misused: *introvert, extrovert, inhibition, repression, expression, sublimation, libido, Oedipus complex, sadism, neuroses.* Religion itself was often looked upon as a neurosis: once a cure for the sick soul, it was now a sign of the soul's sickness. The general conclusion: all restraint is bad, mental health requires a free outlet of sexual impulses.

The impact of Freudian and other psychologies on the literature of the 1920's and 30's was tremendous. A whole new and exciting realm of interpretation was opened up, explored, and occupied, giving fresh impetus to the realistic and naturalistic movement. The analysis of complexes and maladjustments bulks large in the fiction of Sherwood Anderson (e.g. *Winesburg, Ohio*, 1919, *Dark Laughter*, 1925), in the plays of the leading American dramatist, Eugene O'Neill (*The Emperor Jones*, 1920, *Strange Interlude*, 1928), in the poems of Robinson Jeffers (*Tamar*, 1924, *Roan Stallion*, 1925). Few if any writers were untouched by the current explanations of human nature.

Revolt of the Intellectuals. In the just-named works by Anderson, O'Neill, and Jeffers; in the novels of Theodore Dreiser, Sinclair Lewis, and Ernest Hemingway; in the poems of T. S. Eliot, and in the essays and editorials of H. L. Mencken, the vague mood of disillusionment and revolt that pervaded the Jazz Age became more clear, conscious, and programmatic.

The critical spokesman was the rampaging H. L. Mencken. A raucous and hard-boiled journalist with a Germanic frankness and combativeness, a keen and ribald sense of humor, a tremendous gusto, and a talent for devastating phrase-making, he made short work of civilization in these United States. He despised the "mob," mercilessly ridiculed the middle class, scorned the aristocratic pretensions of the plutocracy. Waving the banner of the German philosopher Nietzsche, he damned both religion and democracy, proclaimed an aristocracy of intelligence, and demanded the right of the elite to live as they pleased and to be amused by the great American circus, an uproarious exhibition of ignorance, stupidity, bigotry, stuffiness, hypocrisy, sentimentalism. To a generation determined to be emancipated, to those who dimly and not always wisely desired a free, creative individualism, he spoke with the authority of a messiah in the pages of the *American Mercury* and the series of books named *Prejudices.* Here his countless readers learned that the grand evil bedeviling American civilization was the tyranny of "Puritan" or "Victorian" repression, epithets used by him and his followers more as swear-words than as historical symbols. The Puritan bogy stood for almost everything that the new elect did not like in the American heritage and environment. Yet much that Mencken said was just and needed saying, and unquestionably he played an important role in preparing the public mind and taste for acceptance of the vital prose fiction coming from the pens of Dreiser, Anderson, and Lewis. Appropriately enough, Lewis dedicated one of his novels "To H. L. Mencken, with profound admiration."

Sinclair Lewis's *Main Street,* published in 1920, was rated by P. W. Slosson, a historian at the end of the Jazz Age, as "the most important book written in the United States in the postwar decade," though several of Lewis's later books were much better novels. Gifted like Mencken with high spirits and a flair for satire, he also wrote with powers of close observation and vivid mimicry that his journalistic champion did not possess. Americans in a mood of vague disenchantment were suddenly given a sharply defined picture — all true if not all the truth — of a typical town, a Main Street that extended clear across the prosperous country. "This is America," said Lewis: "an unimaginatively standardized background, a sluggishness of speech and manners, a rigid ruling of the spirit by the desire to appear respectable. It is contentment . . . the contentment of the quiet dead, who are scornful of the living for their restless walking. It is negation canonized as the one positive virtue. It is the prohibition of happiness. It is slavery self-sought and self-defended. It is dullness made God."

Attached to his country, cherishing what H. S. Canby called "a fierce idealism for America," Lewis had brooded long upon the dismal reality achieved by a triumphant middle class, upon the symptoms of the Main Street virus that had infected village, town, and city. He described it again in later books, most notably in *Babbitt,* in which the central character, a realtor, comes dimly to see the American way of life for what it is: "Mechanical business — a brisk selling of badly built houses. Mechanical religion — a dry, hard church, shut off from the real life of the streets, inhumanly respectable as a top hat. Mechanized golf and dinner parties and bridge and conversation. Save with Paul Riesling, mechanical friendships — back-slapping and jocular, never daring to essay the test of quietness." In such a society, intellectually and emotionally starved, inwardly insecure despite its complacency and demand for conformity, there could be only the shadow of culture, typified by the silly "Thanatopsis Club" in *Main Street.* The creative mind, Lewis seemed to be saying, must either accept frustration or make its escape.

In actual life many of the creatively minded escaped to a Bohemian freedom in one of the large cities, preferably New York. There the district known as Greenwich Village, ever since the turn of the centry, had been attracting young writers and artists with or without talent. They could live cheaply in hall bedrooms or attics, and enjoy independence, companionship, and love accompanied by some work and much gay Prohibition drinking. Hither came Eugene O'Neill, getting into his stride as a playwright, Edna St. Vincent Millay, red-haired, sophisticated innocent, darling of flappers everywhere, and the shy and ardent Floyd Dell, who in *Moon-Calf* and other novels spoke for young lovers seeking happiness in the machine age. In his *Love in Greenwich Village* a modern wife leaves her husband because he wants her to sew buttons on his shirts — "I've got a right to be *myself,*" she said.

Or one could escape the dull mechanism of American life altogether by taking refuge in Europe. Seeking richer cultural currents, T. S. Eliot had been living in England since 1914 and in the 1920's became a British subject. Ezra Pound had gone abroad still earlier, sojourning in Spain, Italy, England, France. But after the war, when exchange rates were favorable, scores of American writers drifted over the Continent, many of them for five years or more, often doing little beyond trying to endure life. They were enticed, above all, to Paris, the center of Bohemianism and of modern artistic and literary experiments. They foregathered on the Left Bank, eating, drinking, adventuring in love or mere sex, doing some writing, meeting other free spirits, wandering from the Café du Dôme to the Cupole and other sidewalk cafés ("Let's go somers and do somethin"). A few were privileged to enter the apartment of the great James Joyce, Irish author of *Ulysses* (published in Paris in 1922 but not legally admitted to the United States till a dozen years later), or to present themselves at the salon of Gertrude Stein, Pennsylvania-born oracle who exerted a strong influence on Hemingway and other writers.

With her aid the low-toned style which Anderson had worked out became in Hemingway's prose the last refinement of sophistication, a primitivistic flatness and bareness, superficially ridiculed later in a *Life* cartoon. *Parent*: "Is your school up to date?" *Teacher*: "Indeed — we're asking Hemingway to write the primer!" One sees the point; yet the famous "Hemingway style," widely imitated, was an achievement of the most delicate art as well as a symbol of the nakedness of spirit brought by disillusion. For a picture of the Lost Generation one can go to *The Sun Also Rises,* a novel in which Hemingway described a group of American and English expatriates, pleasure-loving but dismally frustrated writers and artists, examples of the spiritual wreckage of the war. The book came out in 1926. The next year a young American, flying alone across the Atlantic in a single-motored plane, landed in Paris and electrified the world. Lindbergh had brought *The Spirit of St. Louis,* and with it the unconquerable spirit of man. With excited admiration and happiness the American people saw the reality of such ideal qualities as they had been debunking. Then they gradually relapsed into their conventional dullness, while the rebels of Greenwich Village and the Left Bank once more made a convention of unconventionality. One heroic act could not remedy the malady of the twentieth-century mind.

It is time to look a little more closely at this malady. What caused the intellectual class to fall into disillusionment, pessimism, and despair, the sense of futility, the grim philosophy of naturalism? Not the World War; it only intensified the crisis of the human spirit. The crisis had taken form, we will remember, with the impact of evolutionary science in the previous century. Could the Christian religion survive? Could a new outlook on the world satisfy the mind and provide the values that make life worth living? Many espoused the religion of Progress. But in the new century this too disintegrated, first in Europe, then in the United States. In 1918, when the old slogan *Progress is the Law of Life* was belatedly inscribed over the door of a legislative chamber in the new Missouri capitol, the American book of the year, among intellectual readers, was the disillusioned and pessimistic *Education of Henry Adams*. Looking backward, Adams conceived of the thirteenth century as "the point of history when man held the highest idea of himself as a unit in a unified universe." Since that medieval century, as every educated person knew, science had taken a series of steps that might be understood as the degradation of man. Copernicus had dethroned our planet. Darwin had reduced physical man to one form of natural life among myriads. Finally Freud, it seemed, had placed even man's inner life in nature, finding it neither rational nor spiritual but impulsive and sexual. Equally depressing was the behaviorism of Watson, widely heralded in the 1920's, which made man the helpless subject of inherited and "determined" responses. Meanwhile the social scientists were commonly assuming that institutions and moral codes have no inherent or permanent validity but are determined and relative. Even the traditional political faith of America was suspect: "At no period since the French Revolution," said Laski at the close of the 20's, "has there been a skepticism of democracy so profound."

When science and scientism were busily deflating the dignity of man, it is scarcely surprising that innumerable thinking people no longer took seriously the Christian view of man or held the churches competent to guide men's morals. But instead of asserting disbelief in Christian doctrine, as many intellectuals had done through the ages, they did something far more devastating: they simply ignored it. They dismissed it with the bland assurance of many undergraduates objecting to chapel: "No intelligent person believes in God any more." What can an intelligent person believe? The typical answer was well indicated by Lee Wilson Dodd in a poem of 1927 addressed to Alexander Pope ("You sang," said Dodd, "Whatever Is, Is Right"):

> . . . our Critics and our Highbrows vie
> In proving Life is worthless, Love a lie,
> All Aspiration a mechanic thrust
> Toward power, an eddy of the soulless dust;
> All Goodness but desire inhibited,
> And Death a meaningless satire on the dead.
> Man's a contraption, they assert, who came
> To consciousness by accident, whose flame
> Is but a tiny spark struck from the flinty breast
> Of Nature by the friction of unrest:
> A spark, 'tis true, that knows itself to be
> A spark — yet quails before mortality;
> A foolish spark, whose self-awareness gains
> It nothing but illusion, passing pains,
> Mere transient pleasures, throe or throb or trance,
> Amid th' electrons' unintentioned dance.

But could science itself be trusted? When the intellectuals arrayed themselves on the side of science against religion, they soon found themselves troubled. They saw that many scientists had fallen into grave doubts about scientific determinism. They saw the certainty which they had associated with science fading away when Whitehead reported that "the simple security of the old orthodox assumptions [concerning matter, space, time, and energy] has vanished," or when Eddington admitted that an "all-engrossing topic" among scientific specialists was "the desperate state of their ignorance." And they saw that they could not grasp and use Einstein's pivotal theory of relativity much more fruitfully than the man in the street who chuckled over the popular limerick:

> There was a young lady named Bright,
> Who could travel much faster than light;
>> She went out one day
>> In a relative way
> And came back the previous night.

The modern mind had rejected the mysteries of religion and looked to science for clear truth, only to find science itself becoming mysterious and elusive. At this juncture, attention was arrested by the appearance in translation (1926-28) of an imposing German work. *The Decline of the West,* by Spengler, a philosophical pessimist, announcing the doom of Western civilization. Many reflective people solemnly asked whether science, a great constructive force in the nineteenth century, was to become a great destructive force in the twentieth. Soon after came an American book, *The Modern Temper,* by Joseph Wood Krutch, an excellent statement of the predicament of those who found in science the only light of the world. Krutch was plainly restive under "the tyranny which scientific thought has come to exercise over the human spirit," — "science, once so much loved but now so much feared." Yet as a candid pessimist he could see only "such despair as must inevitably be ours."

The Quest of Values

Humanism and Religion. The collapse of the Big Boom in the fall of 1929 shattered the Roaring Twenties. The long weekend party was over, and the revellers and pessimists sobered in the cold gray light of the Great Depression, deepest and longest in American history. The external events beginning with Franklin Roosevelt's time are perhaps too generally familiar to be rehearsed here. But we may outline the internal events — the changing interests of the public and the interpretation of experience by a variety of critical and creative minds.

Critical and creative minds faced a new situation in the decade of the Depression. The irresponsible mood of the 20's was now passé. It was time to find — or to grope earnestly toward — values and standards that might once more make sense of life. The dark fears that beset the 30's must be countered by objects of hope and loyalty. This call to order and faith did not, of course, come suddenly. As grimly naturalistic literature still had a place in the 30's, so the quest for values had had a place in the 20's. Novels like Willa Cather's *Death Come for the Archbishop* (1927), Thornton Wilder's *The Bridge of San Luis Rey* (1927), poems like those of Robert Frost in the 20's and earlier, and Stephen Vincent Benét's *John Brown's Body* (1928) anticipated the new mood of disillusion with disillusionment. Perhaps it is also significant that in the very heart of the age of jazz, gin, and sex the best selling book of 1926 (more than a million copies, surpassing even the popular novels) was Will Durant's *Story of Philosophy*.

The basic need of modern man lay in the realm of moral philosophy, according to Walter Lippmann, influential columnist and author of a number of respected books. In *A Preface to Morals,* published 1929 in an edition of 80,000 copies, Lippmann showed how modernity had dissolved the religious tradition and brought "moral anarchy within and without." Emancipation had finally led the postwar generation to "disillusionment with their own rebellion," to the discovery that "there is no freedom in mere freedom." But a return to the old religion Lippmann regarded as impossible. Instead, he called for a "philosophy of life" founded on insight into human nature and clarifying the relation of freedom and restraint. The approach to such a philosophy would be that employed in "the literature and thought of the past," i.e. "introspection, general observation, and intuition." Help could also be derived from the concepts of psychology and from the objective frame of mind developed by modern science and industry. But Lippmann's effort to show how the malady of the age might be remedied was less impressive than his diagnosis.

Meanwhile, critics, scholars, and journalists were taking sides in a hot controversy over humanism. For many years Irving Babbitt, Paul Elmer More, and their followers had been building up the first serious attack on current trends in thought and literature. Their work had been largely ignored until about 1928, when the gathering reaction against the excesses of the 20's made it more pertinent. For more than two years the embattled humanists assailed the intellectual status quo in a number of books (including a concerted manifesto) and in such periodicals as the *Bookman* and the *Forum,* while the defenders multiplied till they reached small-town newspapers. Humanists were pictured as outdated Classicists, Puritans, and bluestockings, while Mencken classed them with "honorary pall-bearers of letters — bogus Oxford dons, jitney Matthew Arnolds." Despite much misrepresentation and confusion, the controversy did succeed in turning attention to more fundamental questions than those which had engaged the 1920's.

Irving Babbitt, at the center of the controversy, held that unless there was "a reaffirmation of the truths of the inner life in some form — traditional or critical, religious or humanistic—" civilization was "threatened at its base." Modernism had put man into nature, first emotionally (Rousseau, Wordsworth), then physically (Darwin), then in every way (Spencer, Freud). But were there not elements in human experience that refused to fit into this scheme? Was there not something distinctively human, a "law for

man" as well as a "law for thing"? Babbitt described it as a
power of self-restraint, of imposing a limit to the flow of appetite
and temperament, of selecting human ends to be served. This
power he attributed not to reason or feeling but to will. He distinguished between a "higher will" and mere impulse, as love
is distinguished from sex. Its effect was to concentrate man's
energies, to bring them to the center of his being. It required
moderation, proportion. It aimed — to state it in familiar terms —
at the centered and well-rounded life often praised in college cata-
logues but often lacking in college graduates. The concept is also
familiar in religion, where the higher will merges into the will of
God. As a critical modern, Babbitt stopped short of the divine
realm; yet he acknowledged the need of humility toward something felt to be above man, and in the debate between naturalists
and supernaturalists did not hesitate to range himself with the
supernaturalists. While never a mere traditionalist, he nourished
himself upon the "wisdom of the ages" — not only the humanistic
doctrine of Aristotle and Confucius but the religious insight of
Jesus and especially Buddha.

T. S. Eliot, when a student at Harvard, had been impressed
with Professor Babbitt's attack on the subjection of man to nature
in the sentimental and scientific forms of humanitarianism. As
the author of *The Waste Land* (1922) he pictured the desolation
wrought by the skeptical temper, the inner emptiness of life without faith. Then in 1927 he announced his conversion to Anglo-
Catholicism. In an essay of this time he held that humanism depends on religion. "For us," he added, "religion is of course
Christianity." He regretted that Babbitt could not take the same
step he had taken: "Professor Babbitt knows too much," "knows
too many religions and philosophies . . . to be able to give himself to any." Holding that humanism needs religion, he also held
(in the humanist manifesto of 1930) that religion needs humanism. Both the Roman Catholic and the Protestant churches, when
lacking humanistic criteria, he pronounced liable to "corruption,"
"stupidity," and "vulgarity." One wing of Protestantism, furthermore, tended to be "liberal, sloppy, hypocritical, and humanitarian." While announcing himself as a believer in Christian revelation, Eliot also announced himself as a classicist. What classicism
meant to him he had already indicated in the year after *The Waste
Land,* when he contrasted it with romanticism: it was complete

not fragmentary, adult not immature, orderly not chaotic. Accepting both the Christian and the classical disciplines, Eliot rejected the postwar skeptical emancipation, which had brought only a "meager, impoverished emotional life; in the end it is the Christian who can have the more varied, refined and intense enjoyment of life."

The return of typically modern minds to the Christian fold had seemed all but impossible ten years earlier. Yet here was Eliot — with a modern sensibility and artistic method that made him a commanding influence on the poets of his time — finding his essential meanings in revealed religion. Nor was this a merely private matter: it provided the substance of his public verse. With *Ash Wednesday* in 1930, Eliot became a Christian poet. So complex a person could not be expected to repeat in the twentieth century the utter certitude of Dante or simple piety of Chaucer. His choice of a Lenten theme for his sequence of six poems itself suggests the modern temper of his faith. He is concerned with self-examination and discipline, with temptation, doubt, penitence, renunciation, prayer, acutely aware of all the tensions of the inner life and the elusiveness of genuine affirmation. Poetry of this sort, interfused with religious dogma and ritual, caused consternation among many of his followers, who now regarded him as a lost leader. Others deplored his retreat to tradition and authority while they admired his craftsmanship. But there were also those who pursued a course of reading and reflection suggested by his own example. As S. I. Hayakawa said in 1934, "He restored theology to us as a living subject so that, perhaps for the first time in a hundred years, it has been no uncommon thing for young literati here and there throughout America to discuss in perfect seriousness such subjects as Grace, Redemption, Original Sin, and Sacramentalism."

Toward the Left. To the religionist or humanist, the fundamental conflict is between good and evil within the human heart. To the ordinary modernist it is between the individual and society. Generally speaking, the nineteenth century was individualistic, and the twentieth has been socialistic. In the United States, the results of free enterprise (when kept within bounds by government) proved so pleasing to all classes that the individualistic pattern was by no means abandoned even by the reforming New

Deal. This is perhaps clearer today than it was during what might be called the Decade of Unemployment.

The Great Depression that spanned the whole of the 1930's seemed to offer an ideal chance for the growth of socialism. There were American roots to begin with. Ever since the days of Populism, political progressives and labor leaders had tended to propagate socialist theories and attitudes, with aid from such novelists as Upton Sinclair (especially in *The Jungle,* 1906), Jack London (*Martin Eden,* 1909), then Floyd Dell and Ernest Poole, as well as such poets as Sandburg and Lindsay. In the 1920's, as we have seen, skepticism of democracy was widespread; even a humorist like Will Rogers lost no opportunity to ridicule the people's Congress. Finally the soil was well prepared by the panic of 1929, the terrifying bank crisis in 1933, the specter of Fascism looming up in Mussolini's Italy, then in Hitler's Germany. Could the ills of American democracy be cured by some simple patent medicine? Could the body politic be restored to health by one or two acts of Congress? Vast numbers of Americans began to suspect that a more heroic regimen was needed. A poll of nearly 20,000 ministers in 1934 revealed that a third of them were ready for the plunge into socialism. Could not the best hints for a new beginning be derived from a great people across the seas, with a planned economy and full employment, moving by Five-Year Plans toward a happy, classless, peaceful society? While tempted by the example of Communist Russia, many Americans hesitated or drew back. Many others hoped that such blessedness could be attained, without violence, by gradual evolution. A much smaller number deliberately warmed their hearts at the fire of Marxism and determined to spread the flames of revolution. Something of the spirit of that day may be found at the end of the *Autobiography of Lincoln Steffens,* goateed veteran muckraker, to whom American evolution was less attractive than Russian revolution "ruthlessly" carried out by "a few thoughtful, feeling individuals." "Not the cunning, grasping possessors of things but the generous, industrious producers and the brave, imaginative leaders of the race shall be the fit to survive. Russia is the land of conscious, wilful hope."

The creative writers of the period had varying attitudes toward American failure and Russian hope, but most of them shared a sense of social sympathy and responsibility, as usual in the 1930's as rare in the 20's. They were ready to hail "the Century of the

Common Man." No longer ridiculed as a boob or yokel, the common man was looked upon as a martyr, a victim of social forces beyond his control. A "Leftist" or "Proletarian" stand was evident in the little magazines such as the *Partisan Review,* in the theater (even Broadway), in such poets as Kenneth Fearing and Muriel Rukeyser, in critics like Granville Hicks and Edmund Wilson. It was no time for a "high society" novelist like Edith Wharton, who complained: "The demand is that only the man with the dinner pail shall be deemed worthy of attention." An anthology, *Proletarian Literature in the United States* (1935), contained stories by sixteen contributors, the most resolutely proletarian being Albert Maltz, Albert Halper, Robert Cantwell, Josephine Herbst — unfamiliar names today. The Communist Party of the United States, thriving in the 1930's, warmly endorsed writing about the working class, drearily approved ill-written representations of "the class struggle." In a lighter vein a company of garment workers produced a musical revue, *Pins and Needles,* which had a record-breaking run and contained a catchy air with the title "Sing Me a Song of Social Significance"!

The better writers who pictured the plight of the common man were only briefly, if at all, Stalinists; rather they were independent Marxists, idealists who felt that the principles underlying Communism held great hope for the world. As better writers, they subdued their radical opinions to their concern for artistic construction. One was James T. Farrell, author of the powerful *Studs Lonigan* trilogy of novels (1932-35) on the degeneration of an Irish Catholic youth in the lower middle class of Chicago, victim of a brutal environment in the depression period. Another was John Steinbeck, whose best-selling novel *The Grapes of Wrath* (1939) pictured the Joad family of the Dust Bowl, tractored off their Oklahoma farm and lured in their jalopy to the uncertain promise of California, a family unquenchable in their love of life, resolute in the face of utter defeat. Plainly, the American Dream that had drawn generations of pioneers westward had turned into a nightmare.

The immediate American past was the subject of one of the most impressive literary achievements of the decade — *U.S.A.* (1930-37), a trilogy of novels by John Dos Passos. It is a panoramic view of the life of America for thirty years, from the pre-war time to the onset of the depression. Samples of public events, great and trivial, are flashed before us in headline fashion, famous leaders like Wilson, Debs, Morgan, Ford, and Hearst are scrutinized in thumbnail biographies, but the bulk of the work is fiction, the stories of a number of diverse men and women. In these characters are few signs of virtue; instead, a monotony of greed, cruelty, lust, drunkenness, bribery, and general cussedness. They can control neither themselves nor their circumstances. Those who strive and those who drift are alike swept to defeat by the destructive forces of society. The author's desire to be honest and forthright seems to lead him to a naturalistic determinism, the judgment that man is hopeless and life futile. Yet Dos Passos loved life and land enough to condemn them in more than 1400 pages, enough to desire a socialist revolution (while looking askance at Communists and other radicals), and enough to later write a book offering men like Jefferson, Franklin, and Roger Williams as *The Ground We Stand On* (1941).

Actually, the case for any sort of violent revolution was undermined by the New Deal. This was much the largest step in a peaceful revolution begun by the Populists and propagated by Bryan, Theodore Roosevelt, La Follette, and finally the greatest of the series, Franklin D. Roosevelt. *That Man,* as big business called the four-term President, made it clear that the day of "economic royalists" was over and with it much of the old individualist philosophy. Under his bold and buoyant leadership, the term *liberal* no longer signified leaving individuals as free as possible to control themselves, it now meant extending social controls over individuals for the general welfare. The Democratic party, though traditionally associated with states' rights, sponsored a vast increase in centralized Federal government. Measure after measure was introduced that had the effect of tying the national economy, from big business down to "the forgotten man," far more closely to Washington. Bureaucracy developed apace; the population of the capital shifted from fourteenth among the cities in 1930 to ninth in 1940; the public debt mounted from $16 billion to $42 billion.

Part of the money was spent in support of artists and writers. Needy painters were employed to adorn the walls of post offices and other Federal buildings with pictures of the Dust Bowl, sharecroppers, strikes, bread lines, etc., sometimes given a Marxist turn under the inspiration of Mexican mural artists, Orozco and

Rivera. Thousands of musicians were aided and more than 100,-000,000 heard their concerts, which included the modern American music of such composers as Copland and Creston. The Federal theater project supported thousands of actors, who put on stage dramatizations of the slum problem, the TVA, the farmers' troubles, and the threat of Fascism (Sinclair Lewis' *It Can't Happen Here* in play form). And another Federal project gave novelists, poets, journalists, and other writers a chance to go on writing. The most notable result of this literary project was a long series of detailed guide books to cities, states, and rivers, with attention to history, folkways, scenery, and practical information, which opened up our widespread and varied country as never before.

Regionalism and the South. The New Deal not only sponsored this inventory of the parts that made the whole, but set up various regional administrative units and ventured a regional experiment involving seven states — the Tennessee Valley Authority. Yet its dominant tendency was plainly toward centralization, as many thoughtful Americans saw with growing alarm. They had shared in the revolt of the prosperous 20's against Main Street and all the dull uniformities of the machine age. Was there not now, in the depressed 30's, grave danger that an ever-increasing mechanical unity resting on Federal authority would in time completely destroy the organic diversity of the United States, a diversity resting on spontaneous differences in interests, customs, ways of looking at life? A spirited controversy arose. Whether regionalism could and should be fostered was discussed by critics, creative writers, journalists, and scholars. Usually those who called themselves regionalists rejected the old term *sectionalism*, which seemed separatist and aloof, while *regionalism* implied the contribution of the parts to the whole. The new term had rather specific meanings when applied to literature and the arts. A representative statement, written in 1937 by the painter Grant Wood for a university graduate class in literature, observed that "in this country, regionalism has taken the form of a revolt against the cultural domination of the city (particularly New York) and the tendency of metropolitan cliques to lay more emphasis on artificial precepts than on more vital human experience." At the same time "it has been a revolt against cultural nationalism — that is, the tendency of artists to ignore or deny the fact that there are important differences, psychologically and otherwise, between the various regions of America. But this does not mean that Regionalism, in turn, advocates a concentration on local peculiarities; such an approach results in anecdotalism and local color."

Definitions and theories of regionalism did little more than rationalize a deep impulse at work in American literature since the rise of realism after the Civil War. The section of the United States that was most distinctive, and most wanted to be itself, had been for four years known as the Confederate States of America. Impoverished in those desperate years, resentful of the horrors of "Reconstruction," the South was long bewildered in its need for refinding itself — not restoring what had been shattered but creating a new economic and social order. It could not forget its own tradition when that tradition, notwithstanding slavery, contained so much that was admirable and charming; nor could it heartily adopt the modern industrial pattern, when this seemed (not without reason) so dubious an avenue to true fulfillment. Some Southerners faced toward the proud past, others accepted what the machine age promised, while many others looked both ways, hoping that an uncertain future would reconcile old and new. Increasingly divided, Southerners agreed at least in devotion to the region and the nation.

Even that boorish newspaperman, H. L. Mencken, Baltimorean born and bred, was attached to the South — the old South, with a civilization "perhaps the best that the Western Hemisphere has ever seen," original in political ideas, accomplished in culture and the art of living. The New South — the South ruined by the Civil War and fallen into the clutches of plutocrats and Protestant barbarians — he pronounced "almost as sterile artistically, as the Sahara Desert" (*Prejudices,* second series, 1920). Had Mencken been a more alert journalist he might have suspected that the desert was about to blossom with talent and genius. An editor of the *American Mercury,* he presently found himself publishing, in the first two years of the magazine, fifty-five contributions by twenty-three Southern writers. And by the end of the 1920's writers of unmistakable genius, as we shall note later, had arisen to place the South in the forefront of American literature.

At the opening of the 1930's, just before the American way of life seemed discredited by the deepening Depression, twelve Southerners issued a critical manifesto entitled *I'll Take My Stand.*

They took their stand in favor of a "Southern way of life against what may be called the American or prevailing way": "Agrarian *versus* Industrial." Agriculture, they said, is "the best and most sensitive of vocations," nourishing social amenities, religion and the arts. They called upon the younger Southerners, led astray by an alien industrial gospel, to "come back to the support of the Southern tradition." Unfortunately, according to the historian of *The South in American Literature,* Jay B. Hubbell, "Their Old South was too much like the idealized picture in Page's *In Ole Virginia."* Among the contributors were John Crowe Ransom, Donald Davidson, Allen Tate, and Robert Penn Warren. They were a brilliant group, natives of Kentucky and Tennessee, who had gathered at Vanderbilt University and written for *The Fugitive,* a magazine of verse. After the agrarian episode, these men attained great distinction as poets without laurels, esteemed by adept readers of "pure" and "obscure" poems but regarded by the general public with indifference or hostility. From this group also came leadership in the "New Criticism," "exclusively," said Ransom, an "aesthetic criticism." The intent of the critic is to examine and define the poem (or prose work of art) with respect to "its structure and its texture." By doctrine and example, Southerners like Ransom, Tate, Warren, and Cleanth Brooks (along with Eliot and other critics in England) exerted a profound influence upon American literary criticism, scholarship, and teaching.

Meanwhile Southern fiction writers, like Southern historical and sociological scholars, were responding to the scientific and realistic temper of the time. Ellen Glasgow, of Richmond, counted in the literary revival as both precursor and participant. She early immersed herself in scientific reading as well as in the English and French realists and naturalists, and reacted against "evasive idealism." After a series of novels on the rise of the middle class in Virginia, she published her most notable work, *Barren Ground,* (1925). Here was no escape to the enchantment of magnolias and mimosas and colonial columns gleaming in the moonlight, but a recognition of the harsh monotony of broomsedge and scrub pine lowlands and the dead weight of poverty and hopelessness that beset agrarian life at "Pedlar's Corner." Through her heroine, Dorinda Oakley, Miss Glasgow showed how sinister conditions could be conquered by intelligence, scientific knowledge, and above all patience and determination. All these qualities were lacking in the degraded human beings — they scarcely seemed human — represented by Erskine Caldwell, a native Georgian, in *Tobacco Road* (1932). The sharecropper Jeeter Lester and his family are incredibly ignorant and shiftless, and they live, in constant hunger, on a plane beneath the moral—a situation to which Caldwell chose to give a comic turn.

To the University of North Carolina, Professor Fred Koch brought from the West his gospel of regional and folk drama. One of his students was Paul Green, whose plays of the 1920's and 30's included *In Abraham's Bosom,* on the Negro problem, and *The House of Connelly,* on the decadence of the planting aristocracy. Another student in the Carolina Playmakers was Thomas Wolfe, who went on to Harvard to write plays in the 47 Workshop, then turned to the novel. In him the South possessed a writer with the vitality of genius, a realist-romanticist whose driving powers got beyond his control. His first novel, *Look Homeward, Angel* (1929), one of the major books of the period, is essentially an account of his own life and family in North Carolina. His later novels, coming out of the depression decade, were also autobiographical, a torrential flow of memories, chants, lamentations: "his loss and loneliness, the furious, irremediable confusion of his huge unrest," as he put it in *Of Time and the River.* Something like his own turmoil he imputed to all America: "Immense and cruel skies bend over us, and all of us are driven on forever and we have no home." Yet he faced life, as Sinclair Lewis said, with great gusto, and, with the hope of the 30's, he loved his America. In the accent of Walt Whitman he exclaims: "I think the true fulfillment of our spirit, of our people, of our mighty land is yet to come." Wolfe early separated himself from the developing literary regionalism of the South, for, though devoted to North Carolina, he could not find there (could he find any-where?) answers to his questions.

The greatest of Southern writers, William Faulkner, lived from childhood days — with few interruptions — in Oxford, Mississippi. Life in "Yoknapatawpha County," a fictional equivalent of Oxford and its surrounding countryside, became the theme of a dozen books that finally brought him international fame. To this immediate theme he gave wide extension: he covered a time span from the early nineteenth century to the present; he implied the experience of the entire South, with its social and moral complexities, its psychological frustrations; and by so doing he suggested the tragic plight of modern man, his soul all but lost in the mechanisms of his religion and his external affairs. His work presents a fearful picture of perversions and acts of violence, till it implies to the casual reader that the abnormal is normal. A great artist, with a blazing imagination, an inexhaustible lyrical responsiveness, a rich fertility in structural devices, he made the most of his horrors. But they grow out of and are sustained by an intense scrutiny of human nature. His horrors, in other words (the words of E. E. Sandeen) "do not occur in the vacuum of mere effects, whether romantic or naturalistic. In fact, his horrors are memorable exactly for the reason that they arouse the sense of moral outrage."

Faulkner's imagination is essentially historical, and the history he contemplated is human, has an ethical center which is permanent and absolute. He felt deeply that the moral law could not be violated by a people or by an individual with impunity. He seemed to think of history as the force which drove his characters, in the manner of the writers of the Old Testament: "The fathers have eaten sour grapes and the children's teeth are set on edge." Like Hawthorne, an artist preoccupied with moral reflection realized aesthetically through symbolism, Faulkner at length turned, in *A Fable* (1954) to a Christian allegory. To his readers in the atomic age he offered this long meditated fable of the premature armistice of 1918, suggesting, behind pacifism, the peace that passeth understanding, the peace of soul without which man is not truly human. The spirit in which he wrote it he had previously made plain enough in his address, in Sweden, upon receiving the Nobel prize:

> I decline to accept the end of man. . . . He is immortal, not because he alone among creatures has an inexhaustible voice, but because he has a soul, a spirit capable of compassion and sacrifice and endurance. The poet's, the writer's, duty is to write about these things. It is his privilege to help man endure by lifting his heart, by reminding him of the courage and honor and hope and pride and compassion and pity and sacrifice which have been the glory of his past. The poet's voice need not merely be the record of man, it can be one of the props, the pillars to help him endure and prevail.